T0332206

What UX Is *Really* About

What UX Is *Really* About
Introducing a Mindset for Great Experiences

Celia Hodent

CRC Press
Taylor & Francis Group
Boca Raton London New York

CRC Press is an imprint of the
Taylor & Francis Group, an **Informa** business

Cover illustration by Laura Taylor.

First edition published 2022
by CRC Press
6000 Broken Sound Parkway NW, Suite 300, Boca Raton, FL 33487-2742

and by CRC Press
2 Park Square, Milton Park, Abingdon, Oxon, OX14 4RN

CRC Press is an imprint of Taylor & Francis Group, LLC

ISBN: 978-1-032-10445-4 (hbk)
ISBN: 978-1-032-10444-7 (pbk)
ISBN: 978-1-003-21537-0 (ebk)

DOI: 10.1201/9781003215370

Typeset in Garamond
by codeMantra

Contents

About the Author

Celia Hodent is an expert in the application of cognitive science and psychology to improve products, systems, services, and video games. She currently leads an independent UX consultancy, working with a wide range of international media and enterprise companies.

She works in-depth with companies to help ensure their products are both engaging and successful by considering the entire user experience (UX) they will provide to their audience. Celia conducts workshops and provides guidance on the topics of game-based UX, playful learning ("gamification"), ethics, implicit biases, and inclusion in tech and video games.

Celia holds a PhD in psychology and has more than 13 years of experience in the development of UX strategy in the entertainment industry, and more specifically with video game studios through her work at Ubisoft, LucasArts, and as Director of UX at Epic Games (*Fortnite*). Celia is the author of *The Gamer's Brain: How Neuroscience and UX Can Impact Video Game Design* (CRC Press, 2017) and *The Psychology of Video Games* (Routledge, 2020).

Introduction: Why Should You Care about UX and This Book?

Have you ever tried to pull a door that needed to be pushed? Or turned on the wrong burner as you wanted to cook dinner? Or struggled to understand how to use a new fancy application on your phone to pay bills? All of these are examples of a bad "user experience" (UX) whereby the user of an object, a system, or a service experiences some friction points (or frustration) that were not intended by its creators. At best, these UX issues are slightly annoying and waste our time. At worst, they can lead to costly or even fatal errors. UX experts are highly trained professionals who strive to anticipate, identify, and fix issues that users of a product may encounter, with the goal to provide the best experience possible and thus increase the likeliness of the product to be successful. This book is a primer into this highly popular yet misunderstood world of UX. You will learn that UX is much more than a set of techniques, guidelines, and tools. It's a mindset; a philosophy that consists of taking the perspective of the humans that will use a product. It's about solving *their* problems, offering them a pleasurable experience, and building a win-win and long-lasting relationship between them and the company developing the product.

If your job is to create a product that will be used by humans, or provide a service to humans, you should care about UX because frustrated users aren't likely to become or remain loyal customers. Caring about the experience you provide to your target audience thus increases your odds of being successful and of your product selling well. And as human beings who use or depend on products all day long, or use systems to entertain ourselves (such as video games), we should all care about having the best experience possible and being respected as a customer or a user. Thus, UX matters to everyone.

The purpose of this book is to provide you with the essential information you need to know about the UX mindset, in a concise and approachable

DOI: 10.1201/9781003215370-1

way. This book is targeted to anyone interested in understanding why certain things are satisfying to use while others are highly frustrating or deceiving. It is not meant for UX professionals or advocates, but for people who have heard of "user experience" and want a better understanding of what it means, or how to get started. Maybe you're looking to apply the UX mindset to your own work, or maybe a UX practitioner has offered you this book so that you can better understand their job and collaborate with them more efficiently. Indeed, offering good UX is a team endeavor, so everyone on the project should at least know the basics. Either way this book is intended for you.

I will give you a high-level tour of UX: what it is (Chapter 1), what it's not and the misconceptions that need debunking (Chapter 2), the origins and science behind the UX mindset (Chapter 3), and its main process and methodologies (Chapter 4). We will also address the ethics, accessibility, and inclusion at the core of this mindset (Chapter 5). Throughout this book, you will discover that UX is fundamentally about improving people's lives with technology.

I hope that you'll enjoy the tour!

1

What Is UX?

Most user experience professionals define UX as a philosophy, an approach, or a mindset. When one uses the term "UX," one implies caring about the *experience* that end *users* have or will have with a product in development, or a product that is already available. This mindset also implies caring for this experience to be the best possible for users, having their best interests in mind, while also minding the business requirements for the product to be viable and profitable (unless it's a not-for-profit endeavor). However, the term UX is often misunderstood, so let's start by defining a few key terms that we will use a lot in this book: user, experience, product, and UX professionals.

1.1 What Is a "user"?

The term "user" generally refers to a human (although animals can also use products made by us) who is interacting with a product, a system, or a service. Thus, the user is not necessarily the customer. If you love video games and you buy one and then play it, you are both the customer and the user. But this is not always the case. If we take the example of a teething toy, the user is typically a baby, while the customer is not (infants are not the ones buying the products). Instead, the customer might be a parent. In many cases, customers' needs are nonetheless aligned with users' needs. In our example, a UX professional will care for the teething toy to be easy to grab by infants and to provide them some relief as they munch on it, which is also what parents care about. However, parents might also care about the aesthetic of the teething toy, while this might not matter as much for the baby.

DOI: 10.1201/9781003215370-2

In some cases, customers' needs might be disconnected to users' or, worse, go against them. For example, users of a social media platform might care about connecting with their friends, while its customers—companies buying advertising space on the platform—care more about making their product visible and encouraging users to engage with their ads and getting their clicks. Users might then end up seeing curated content that will maximize their engagement with ads (customers' goal) rather than reinforce their bonds with their friends (users' goal).

UX professionals care about *users first*. They "fight for the user," so to speak. *All* of the users, not only those who look, think, and behave like them. Having a UX mindset also means caring about inclusion and accessibility. All humans are very similar in most ways, but we are also all a bit different as well. Our small differences are what continue to make humanity so rich and interesting. Accounting for all types of the target users is a key component of UX.

1.2 What Is an "experience"?

The term "experience" refers to what happens when the user interacts with a product, a system, or a service, broadly speaking. Is the interaction intuitive? Do users understand what is going on and what they need to do in order to accomplish their goals? Does this interaction result in satisfying users' needs and is it pleasurable? In this case, an "interaction" entails what users perceive, what they understand, what actions they do, and how the product is responding to these actions. Sometimes, the experience is mostly about perception and understanding. Take a clock. Most of the time and for most people, the experience we have with a clock is merely our visual perception of it and subsequently our understanding of the information conveyed. The size of the clock and how well the numbers contrast with the background will affect how readable it is. We might also understand the information conveyed by the clock better when the time is displayed in a digital way, rather than when it's displayed in an analog way (with hands spinning around a dial) with no numbers at all. At times, we might need to interact physically with the clock, to adjust it for daylight saving for example, or to change its batteries.

An experience has a lot to do with interacting with the product itself (the clock in our example), but not only. UX professionals consider the *entire* experience that led users to interact with the clock: why they wanted a clock, how they bought it (unless the user is not the customer or the product is not-for-profit), how they installed it, how they commonly use it, what happens if there is a problem with it, and they need to contact the customer service. In fact, consideration of the entire *experience* that *users* have during their whole *journey* with a product and its ecosystem is what led Donald Norman, a famous designer and cognitive scientist, to coin the term "UX" in the 1990s. As UX expert Peter Merholz and colleagues say in their book *Subject to Change* (2008), experience is the only thing that users care about. Thus, this is the most important thing that product creators should care about, more than the product itself.

1.3 What Is a "product"?

In this book, I will use the term "product" to refer to anything users interact with to attain goals, or to be entertained. For example, a microwave is a product that many of us use to heat our food. The term product can thus refer to a physical object (e.g. a microwave, a bottle of water, a toy, a screwdriver, a car, a book), or a digital object (e.g. a video game, an e-book, a website, a smartphone application). It can also refer to a system (e.g. the electoral system of a nation, an education system, a travel reservation system), and/or a service (e.g. a customer service, a delivery service, a translation service).

All those products have certain characteristics and features, some of which directly or indirectly interface with the user. For example, the microwave has an integrated timer system, which is a feature that users can control through face buttons (those buttons are part of what we call the "user interface," or "UI"). Domestic microwaves also feature a rotating functionality that is meant to heat the food more evenly (to the delight of the user) but not meant for users to interact with directly (we place the food on the plate, which in turn is connected to the rotating device). In the digital world, a feature that users can directly interact with is qualified as being "front-end" while that which is out of reach is qualified as "back-end." If we take the example of a shopping website, we use the interface (i.e. what we perceive and interact with) to navigate the site, select items, and then buy them. As we do so, in the "back-end" the system is saving the items chosen, consequently adjusting the remaining stock at the warehouse when relevant, communicating with your bank and postal services to seal the purchase, and ship you the items.

At this stage, you might think that having a UX mindset primarily involves technology and requires technical expertise. Many aspects of UX are, in fact, technical. A UX approach requires understanding how a system works in the back-end, how elements should be displayed in the front-end, how humans tend to interact with the system and its surroundings, and overall why they do the things they do. And it often implies understanding how new technologies work and what they can offer. However, one can have a UX mindset for products that aren't high-tech. For instance, if you own and run a food truck, the product you sell to customers (who are often also your users) is food. The food has certain characteristics: its taste, how it's presented, wrapped-up, and whether you can easily carry and eat the food while on the go. Caring about the quality of the product is essential, but a UX mindset also involves caring about why your customers will choose your food truck among all the other options they have, how they will order the food, pay, and how you will manage to reduce their wait time. Caring about your user experience is not only important for tech companies, it's important for any company, and overall anyone offering any type of service.

Having a UX mindset is not just about caring what features (whether back-end or front-end) the product should have, but more importantly it's about caring about *why* people would want this product, how they would use it, if this interaction is intuitive and pleasurable, and finally if the product is satisfying from the user's point of view, considering the entire user journey. Food truck owners care about how people become aware of their business (by smelling delicious food in the street, or seeing an aesthetically pleasing truck, or discovering it out via an application or a leaflet), how they can take notice of the menu and understand it, how they will order the food, how they can eat the food without burning themselves or staining their jacket if they eat on the go, how satisfied they are by the food itself, and if something is wrong with their order, how their complaints are taken care of. And, of course, if everything went well and users are happy, they might spread the word around them and come back regularly.

Caring about the user experience means caring about every little step of the journey that enjoying your product implies. It's caring about the whole experience for all users.

1.4 Who Are the "UX professionals"?

Having a UX mindset means having users' best interests in mind. Therefore, technically, UX should be the concern of everyone in a company or organization who directly or indirectly impacts how users will experience a product. It is not the sole responsibility of people having "UX" in their job title. That being said, UX experts are either trained in the science behind UX (human factors and ergonomics, as discussed in Chapter 3) and/or the process, techniques, or methodology that help advance UX (which we will address in

Chapter 4). To simplify, we can broadly consider three overarching and overlapping categories of UX practitioners:

- "UX designers," who are experts in applying the lessons from the "human-computer interaction" (HCI) field to design a product and its ecosystem.
- "UX researchers," who are experts in conducting studies using the scientific method to understand users and objectively evaluate their experience with a product.
- "UX strategists," who are experts in advocating for UX practices (i.e. "Lean UX" or "design thinking"), managing other UX experts, and establishing a strategy across a team or a company. These professionals are often called "UX principals" or "directors of UX."

This listing is not exhaustive but reflects a categorization of the most common UX professionals currently found today. Other profiles exist and are starting to be more visible, such as UX writers who are responsible for writing copy that will be clear and enjoyable for users. Hopefully, more UX profiles will become popular in the near future.

1.4.1 UX Designers

The term UX designer can be confusing because it suggests that those professionals are designing the experience users will have, and that they are solely responsible for it. However, an "experience" is not something that can be designed because it's the subjective perception and perspective that happens in people's minds as they interact with a product or its ecosystem. What we can design is a specific environment that we hope will provide a certain experience to our target users when they interact with it. This point is key: We don't design an experience; we design *for* an experience. UX designers are experts in designing for an experience by applying HCI principles (see Chapter 3) and using an iterative process (see Chapter 4). Second, UX designers are not solely responsible for the experience users have. Everyone on a product team, the "support teams," and the executives setting the values and general direction for the company all are responsible for it.

UX design designates a generalist role encompassing all the following tasks: understanding users and their needs, generating ideas to solve users' problems (ideation phase), prototyping, testing with actual users, iterating, and refining the design until it's ready for implementation. Although it is common for additional tasks to be assigned to UX designers, the discipline of UX design itself does not inherently involve the implementation of designs. It also does not traditionally involve aesthetics, creative direction, style guides, or branding of a product (which is more typically the role of visual designers). UX design focuses on *why* users should care about the product and *how* it should work. The main role of UX designers is to understand what goals users have, what problems they are facing as they are trying to accomplish goals, and how these problems can be solved. UX designers collaborate with their teammates on the content strategy and scope (i.e. what features the product should have) and are experts in defining the structure and organization of a product (i.e. information architecture) and how users will interact with it (i.e. interaction design). Information architecture is about organizing the content and features of a product to help users understand the product and accomplish their goals as exemplified in the organization of a clothing store. For example, does it make more sense to organize the items by colors, by type (i.e. pants, skirts, shirts, dresses, accessories), or by size? You want to organize your store based on what your clients expect and their goals. Now think of a website or a smartphone application: how do you organize your menu so that users can easily access the features that they mostly need and care about?

Interaction design is about defining how users will interact with a product. In the example of the store, it's thinking about how clients will navigate around the aisles, how they will carry the items they want to try to the booths, and how they will pay. In an app, it's about thinking about users' input to accomplish their goals, such as if they need to do a "swipe" or "tap" gesture to select an item, preventing user errors or helping them recover from them, such as if they selected the wrong item, and determining what feedback to give them in such a case. For example, after pressing the button to a certain floor in an elevator, the button lighting up is feedback informing users that the system has acknowledged the user's input. Interaction design typically involves a UX designer creating low and medium fidelity prototypes to test their assumptions. These prototypes are often made using software that enables non-technical people to quickly create "real" looking interfaces without requiring implementation from an engineer. They are intended to be a high-level representation of the intended design focused on functionality and interaction, without getting caught up in the details of its "look and feel." Lastly, interaction design is about determining how *all* users can interact with the product, including those with disabilities and varied needs or characteristics (such as size, weight, strength, or skin complexion). An automatic soap dispenser should work with both light and dark skins. A seatbelt should equally protect short and tall people. A store should avoid unnecessary stairs or have ramps or elevators to be accessed by wheelchair users. Apps should provide flexible ways to be used by everyone. Thus, identifying and removing all unnecessary barriers to make a product as inclusive as possible is essential to UX. Note that the term interaction design also designates the practice of designing interactive digital products (abbreviated as "IxD," such as in the Association for Interaction Design[1] abbreviated "IxDA") and can be used as a synonym for human-centered design or even UX design in some cases. The term UX design can thus be confusing and is not considered a satisfying term by some people in the UX field. For example, UX designer (and interaction designer) Jonathan Korman points out that the term "UX design" to describe "this thing that we do" often ends up being a catch-all term lacking a clear meaning[2] (Korman, 2012).

As mentioned earlier, visual design is usually outside of the scope of UX designers, yet they're increasingly expected to add this skill to their tool kit as there's a strong common misconception that UX is mostly about visual design. This is why the currently popular term "UI/UX" can be frustrating for many UX designers as it perpetuates the notion that their work is focused on visual design or on UI art (independent of some UX designers enjoying this work), which dismisses their actual core expertise (i.e. solving problems). Instead, part of UX designers' work is to mostly focus on the UI *skeleton*: defining where should elements be placed and what information to give users, ensuring that users can distinguish between interactive elements (e.g. buttons) and non-interactive elements.

Above all, UX designers work on all the aforementioned elements using a specific methodology that places the users at the center of the process, which is called "human-centered design" (see Chapter 4). Very briefly, this methodology entails understanding who the target users and their goals are, and then developing prototypes that are tested with users before iterating further and implementing the design.

1.4.2 UX Researchers (or User Researchers)

The term "user researcher" can also be confusing because it suggests that users are the ones under scrutiny rather than the product in development

---

[1] See IxDA.org and interaction-design.org.
[2] https://boxesandarrows.com/this-thing-that-we-do/.

as tested by researchers, with the help of users. This is why I prefer the term "UX researcher." Broadly speaking, UX researchers are the ones measuring the actual experience users have (i.e. how easy to use and satisfying it is), and verifying the product team's assumptions on users and their goals, and how the product can satisfy these goals (see Chapter 4). When users encounter frustrations with the product, the aim of user research is to define why they are happening and how to fix them. An example of a UX test (or user test) would be to invite someone representative of the target audience to test a prototype or an early version of the product and ask them to accomplish a specific task while the research team observes. The goal is to determine if the product is intuitive to the target audience or if users encounter friction points (i.e. "UX issues") using objective measures, such as the number of mistakes made by users, the time needed to accomplish a task, and if the task was completed. This method allows comparing what the development team *intended* to do with what users *actually* experience.

While UX designers can sometimes run their own testing, user researchers are specifically trained in conducting research in the most objective way possible, which is much harder than it sounds. Humans are flawed and biased by nature, and we mostly don't realize that we are. Conducting research is about measuring a phenomenon in such a way that the findings aren't tainted by unrelated or unconsidered factors. For example, if you are designing a website and you ask a friend to try it out and give you feedback, chances are that your friend won't want to hurt your feelings. Thus, even if they are trying to be objective to give you useful feedback, they most likely won't be able to. For example, they might try harder to understand how to accomplish a task than if they were using a website from someone they don't know. Also, the people who are participating in the development of a product are not the best ones to conduct user research as they might unwillingly bias how the study is run. They might inadvertently ask leading questions such as "Did you find the interface easy to use?" thus influencing testers to answer positively, regardless of their actual experience.

UX researchers are trained in determining the adequate research methodology, designing rigorous experimental protocols, preparing and running the study, collecting data, and analyzing results without introducing any biases, or at least by controlling for them. This is broadly what we call "the scientific method," a standardized and rigorous way of acquiring knowledge. User researchers are typically graduates from social or cognitive sciences and know how to run academic research. While academic research is much more rigorous than user research, the latter requires a fast turnaround to improve a product before its release date. UX researchers are expected to provide insights into where problems encountered by users are coming from, and suggestions for how to fix these issues.

In the overarching category of research we can include data scientists, who are often closely collaborating with user researchers: they, too, explore how users interact with the product but more often via "telemetry" data (i.e. data collected remotely). They also use a rigorous methodology to make sense of the data collected, but they deal with a much bigger data set. User researchers typically (but not exclusively) conduct qualitative research with a small number of potential users who directly interact with the product in development, while data scientists typically (but not exclusively) conduct quantitative research remotely with a large number of actual users after the product is released. Other types of studies can be conducted, such as elaborating and sending out a survey to a medium or large sample of users.

1.4.3 Directors of UX (or UX Strategists)

UX professionals often reach the point in their career when they manage a team, coordinate UX efforts, participate in advancing the UX maturity at a company, or develop the UX strategy for a product or a brand (see Chapter 4). These professionals interface with the heads of other teams (e.g. development team, marketing team, business intelligence team) and executive managers (or they can themselves be an executive manager in companies with advanced UX maturity). They ensure that everyone is aligned regarding what experience is intended for whom, that the company is staffed appropriately and has adequate processes, and that executive decisions are enlightened by proper analysis of the data available and are ethical. The role of UX director or strategist is often how many UX professionals evolve in a company, and it can later evolve into a "UX principal" or "Vice President of UX" role in the most UX-mature companies.

1.5 A Definition of UX

User experience is best seen as a mindset. It's about shifting from the subjective and necessarily biased point of view of the small number of people working on a product and its ecosystem, to adopt the point of view of all potential users (the "target audience") with the intention of offering them the best experience possible all throughout their journey by taking into account human capabilities and limitations, while having their best interests in mind.

While UX professionals do need to take into account a certain number of constraints, such as the budget limitation, time and workforce available to develop the product, and the business model, their primary goal is to strive to put the interests of users first. They do so by using cognitive science knowledge, HCI principles, and an iterative design cycle (i.e. "design thinking") using the scientific method (i.e. UX research) to verify any assumptions.

I like to describe the UX mindset as requiring *all* of the following pillars (Figure 1.1):

1. UX is human-centered.
2. UX is grounded in science.
3. UX is a team-based process.
4. UX is benevolent.

FIGURE 1.1
UX Mindset Pillars (human-centered, grounded in science, team-based process, benevolent). (Illustration by María Capel.)

- **Having a UX mindset implies being human-centered** (i.e. placing the users at the center of what we do). We don't just assume that people will need certain features or will want to accomplish certain goals in a particular way with the product we are developing. We actually try to understand users, look at what issues they encounter, ask them what they think, and empathize with their needs. The goal is to identify problems that users have and ensure that the product will efficiently solve or address those specific problems. A UX process cannot happen without actual users.

- **Having a UX mindset implies having a scientific approach**. UX professionals stay away from battles of opinions. Instead, we use science: cognitive science knowledge and HCI principles guide us, and we use the scientific method in our research. We start with hypotheses, such as "adding this feature and designing it this way should alleviate some frustration for users when they need to accomplish a specific task" and then test the assumption as objectively as possible while controlling for biases. We collect data (e.g. observation, experimentation, telemetry data) to validate whether our assumptions are correct or not. If not, we conduct more research to identify why the product is failing to accomplish its goals and how to fix it. HCI principles are very useful to avoid common pitfalls, but each product is different and caters to different users having different needs. We do not rely on opinions; we rely on analyses conducted on data carefully collected with actual users to answer to defined hypotheses. A UX process cannot exist without a scientific approach to solving problems for users.

- **Having a UX mindset *is* a process resulting from the efforts of a team**; it is not one step of the process conducted by one expert. UX requires the entire product team (as well as operations team and other support teams) to coordinate around understanding users and their goals, prototyping, testing, and iterating to get as close to perfection from the users' point of view as possible. For *all* users. It means that we constantly need to evaluate and adjust our designs, especially for applications and live services that will never cease to evolve.

- **Having a UX mindset is about being benevolent** (i.e. caring for users' best interests). While UX professionals need to account for production and business constraints, they care about users' best interests first. They strive to improve people's lives by making usable and pleasurable products for users that will be profitable for businesses while minding for inclusion, accessibility, and ethics. A happy and respected user makes a happy and loyal customer; it's a win-win situation both for users and businesses. This fourth pillar is the most important one, because it states the purpose and intention behind the UX mindset.

If any one of these pillars is missing during the development of a product, then it cannot be called a UX approach.

2

What UX Is Not

With UX becoming trendy, misconceptions have been flourishing and spreading. Let's address the main misconceptions about UX and debunk them.

2.1 UX Is Not about Manipulating Users at Their Expense to Make a Product More Profitable

There's a relatively new misconception considering that UX professionals are serving businesses' interests at the expense of users, and it's a sadly growing sentiment. However, having a UX mindset is the exact opposite of putting a business above users' needs and best interests, as mentioned earlier. You cannot maliciously manipulate users and simultaneously be their advocate. In fact, UX professionals are typically so focused on users that many UX articles and books find it useful to remind them that they need to accomplish their mission while accounting for business goals.

A product is always developed with constraints: time constraints, technical constraints, limited budget, and/or limited workforce. Which is why we cannot spend too much time investigating what users need or what issues they experience because we must make fast decisions so that we don't go over budget or behind schedule (although this is still something that happens in the large majority of cases). We need to have a fast turnaround and to make sure that the costs of production won't be greater than the revenues the product will bring. This is true even when working on a product that is not for profit. Let's say that you're working on a new public service financed by taxpayers, such as building a public school or implementing a fire department in a community, even if this product does not need to make profits, it

DOI: 10.1201/9781003215370-3

still needs to be completed and to fulfill its goals within a certain budget and time, and considering specific resources. No matter whether the product is for profit or not, the UX mindset has to take into consideration economic constraints. In the case of a business, a product that doesn't make enough profits to support the cost of future production or product maintenance will ultimately be discontinued.

However, taking business or economic constraints into consideration does not mean prioritizing business over user needs. Neither does it mean maximizing profits at the expense of users' best interests. In a UX approach, it must be a win-win situation for both the business and users.

Many books, articles, or podcasts claim to explain how to use science (mostly psychology) to "captivate" users, "get them," "hook" them, or "persuade" them to convert into paying customers or to use the platform longer to benefit from advertising revenues. And they will also declare that this is just what doing business is about. These practices actually raise clear ethical concerns (see Chapter 5 on ethics), and they are absolutely not following a UX mindset, even if they sometimes use the same scientific knowledge or methodologies. It's not UX unless the users' best interests are at the forefront of priorities. This is one of the most important pillars of UX. Favoring profits over users, per definition, is betraying the purpose of having a UX mindset. It's as simple as that. UX means caring about making your product inclusive, and accessible to people with disabilities. It means solving problems that your users have and care about, while being respectful of their time, money, and well-being.

2.2 UX Is Not Just "common sense"

Occasionally, some professionals believe that because they have enough seniority or have a good "common sense," they do not need UX professionals or feel that applying a UX practice isn't necessary. Those people might say things like "it's obvious why this isn't working," "I know what our customers want," or "I know why such product was/wasn't successful." These are a mix of several human biases and logical fallacies that can make us too confident, overlook key information, and make bad decisions in the end. Humans have great capabilities, but we are also deeply biased (see Chapter 3, Section 3.2). The "hindsight bias" is among those biases. It's the tendency to forget about our doubts while an event is unfolding and then believing past events are more predictable than they actually are. For example, at the launch of a new product, we might have doubts whether it will be successful or not. But if the product ultimately fails, we can say things like "I knew it all along!" therefore forgetting that we were not actually so sure while the event was unfolding. This bias is likely to make us over-confident in our own skills to predict the success or failure of a product in development, which will make us overlook subtle red flags if we do not have a strong UX process.

Another bias we commonly have is the egocentric bias. It's the tendency to rely too heavily on our own perspective, and believing that others should experience something in the same way we do. When we believe that we understand what our customers want, need, and what they are frustrated about without actually conducting any research with them, then we are fooling ourselves with the egocentric bias. Even if you believe you understand them, your users will always have a different perspective than you. "You are not your users," as UX professionals like to repeat to over-confident coworkers. The UX approach will help you verify your assumptions early on, so that you can correct any mismatch between what experience you perceive your product is offering to your users and what users *actually* experience early enough so that you can correct issues and stay on track.

Common sense is only as good as our current knowledge about a subject. It doesn't account for what we might be overlooking, or for our biases. For example, it was not common sense for physicians to wash their hands in between patients to avoid spreading germs until the late 19th century. We don't know what we don't know. Your common sense won't be able to uncover the areas for which you lack awareness (commonly yet inaccurately called "blind" spots), but a UX process might, especially if you are developing an innovative product and navigating uncharted waters.

2.3 UX Is Not a Synonym of "UI," or about Making Things Beautiful

When talking about UX, many people narrow it down to how the user interface (UI) looks. A UI will greatly affect the experience that users have with a product, but it is not the whole experience. The UI is what users can perceive and interact with, and it is of course very important to get right, but the aesthetic appearance of the UI is not all that is important in UX. A popular example of this among UX blogs is a bottle of ketchup. A glass container might look more aesthetically pleasing to users, but it's not easy to use, especially when the container is half empty and we need to frantically shake it upside down and/or vigorously tap on its bottom to get the ketchup out of it. A plastic container might arguably look less elegant, but it makes the experience of getting the ketchup out much smoother as a gentle squeeze is enough. A glass container has different UI characteristics than a plastic container, and while both visual presentations affect the user's experience differently, *how* we interact with the product has an even greater impact (Figure 2.1). UX is not about making a UI aesthetically pleasing; it's about making an interface *both* usable and pleasurable. And it's not only about considering the interface alone; UX is about considering the whole user journey through a product's lifecycle. For example, a slim plastic mustard container might be easy to use without any other tool, but a wide glass container might be kept by users as a drinking glass once emptied and cleaned instead of just thrown away. People mindful of contributing to the plastic waste issue might prefer the hassle of using a spoon to extract the mustard they need from the container rather than adding more to the landfill (assuming in this case that the user is also the customer buying the product). Ideally, you might want to offer different options to your customers, so that you can cater to different needs, goals, and abilities. Doing so is better for your users but it might be difficult to accomplish in terms of production costs. Listing all of the pros and cons of different design options from the users' perspective so that you can make the design that is the most satisfying both for your users and your business is what having a UX strategy is about. Establishing this strategy is what UX work is truly about.

FIGURE 2.1
The user experience of ketchup containers depending on their interface (UI). (Illustration by Laura Taylor.)

2.4 UX Is Not Just One Step in the Process

UX professionals working in freelance often hear that their services are not required quite yet, and that they will be called once the production team is ready to "UX the product." UX is not a verb; it's not a magic step of the process when all the things that aren't clear for users will easily be identified and understood with a simple test and then magically resolved with a few tweaks. Doing this can only help patch a few smaller issues here and there, but it won't help you create a product that will offer a great experience to users. UX is about placing the end users at the center of what you do at every step of the way. It's about first trying to understand users; what they need, want, and think before even ideating solutions for them. It's about evaluating your ideas and design solutions with your target audience, getting their feedback, and adjusting your prototypes in several iterative cycles before finally implementing your design and keep adjusting it with users' feedback, even until after your product is released in many cases. If you wait too long, until "the product is ready for UX," then it will more than likely be too late to fix any larger usability issues due to cost or the product deadline. UX is not a step in the process; it *is* the process.

2.5 UX Is Not "too expensive"

Companies with a low UX maturity (more about this in Chapter 4) have a tendency to consider the cost of hiring UX experts and applying UX methodologies without fully grasping the benefits, and ultimately savings, they will bring. Of course, if you have a very small company, it can be challenging to invest in UX, just like it will be challenging to invest in marketing or information technology (IT) solutions. However, developing and publishing a product without having UX experts helping out and conducting user tests early can have an important yet invisible cost. Failing the launch of a product because users don't understand how it works or don't understand its purpose can have catastrophic consequences. Thus, good UX is also good business! A UX mindset applied from the early stages of your development process will help you identify issues that you will more easily and cheaply be able to address early on, rather than once the product is in its late stages. UX experts and tools are an investment; they will increase the likelihood of your product to be appreciated and successful. As many UX experts typically say, don't ask yourself if you can afford having a UX mindset, ask yourself if you can afford not to.

2.6 UX Does Not Hamper Creativity

In certain industries, such as the video game industry, there is sometimes a strong sentiment that applying UX practices will muzzle artists' creativity. When the product is about entertainment or is an art form, there's often a fear that science and processes will alter the creative mind. First of all, science and creativity are not antithetical, as pointed out by professor of psychology Anna Abraham in her fascinating book *The Neuroscience of Creativity* (2018). Both scientific and artistic domains foster groundbreaking ideas and discoveries and, contrary to the common myth, both brain hemispheres are involved in creativity. Thus, a scientific process cannot by itself hamper creativity.

Second of all, UX is not just about offering the best experience possible to users; it's also about offering the experience *intended* by creators (as long as this intention is benevolent). If the product is a tool intended to help users accomplish certain goals, UX practices will help accomplish this objective. But a video game is not a tool. Users don't need to interact with such a system to accomplish goals; the whole point is to interact with the system for the sake of it, to have fun. In this case, game UX professionals will not try to remove all the friction points that users (players in this case) can encounter; otherwise just clicking a button should allow you to win a game. The idea then is to remove all the friction points that are *not* by design, not intended by game designers and artists (see Hodent, 2020, for a short overview of how the UX mindset is applied to video games). In these cases, the intended design for players is for them to be able to understand the game, but more importantly to be challenged adequately, have fun, and to feel certain emotions. UX practices will absolutely help you accomplish this goal because it's about providing users the best experience possible and the one *intended* for them. As a matter of fact, Walt Disney is sometimes credited to be one of the early UX designers (e.g. Dickersen, 2013) because of his attention to detail, use of experimental prototypes, and focus on providing a magical and life-improving experience to the audience, like in the design process of Disneyland. As the mantra goes, "the absence of limitations is the enemy of art" (attributed to Orson Welles). UX is about minding the limitations of the humans who will enjoy a product or an art form, and it is thus a powerful tool for creative minds.

2.7 UX Is Not Pointless If the Product Is Already Selling Well

Random chance happens and sometimes a product can be successful despite a lack of UX processes during its development. When this happens, the product team and executives can believe they don't need to change their mindset or process. The problem with this thinking is without a strong UX process, it can be very difficult to sustain success over time, or to replicate success with a new product. Furthermore, it's not because a product makes money that users are entirely satisfied, or that there isn't any room for improvement. A UX mindset will help you think systematically and objectively about your product, ensure it will delight users in the long term (not just shareholders in the short term), and keep you ahead of your competitors who will likely one day come up with a better UX for the same type of product if you rest on your laurels.

2.8 UX Is Not Just the Responsibility of a Few Experts

UX experts bring knowledge and tools to a team to enable UX practices on a project, but they are not solely responsible for the experience users will have in the end. UX should be the concern of everyone on the development team, and everyone at the company.

Having a UX mindset simply means that you care more about what users think of your products than about your own opinion. It's about shifting from our egocentric and biased perspective to adopt the perspective of all users. Beyond its experts, its science, and its tools, UX is a philosophy more than anything.

Now that we've cleared the most common UX misconceptions, let's dive in into the science behind it.

3

The Science Behind UX

3.1 A Short History

The term "user experience" was coined relatively recently (in the 1990s) by Donald Norman. However, its roots are much older and UX can have various appellations depending on the time period, specific disciplines, and professionals. The scientific discipline behind it is called "human factors," and the design practice associated with the UX mindset is usually called "human-centered design" (HCD), although different terms with subtle nuances exist (such as design thinking, user-centered design, interaction design, and UX design). Human factors aim at increasing the "usability" of a product (i.e. ease of use, efficiency, satisfaction), its comfort, security, and even pleasure when humans interact with objects or systems, from tool manipulation, to road safety, to medical safety, to education, and to entertainment … for *all* potential users of the system. The ultimate goal is to increase the quality of life for all humans.

The human factors field is more often called *ergonomics* in Europe and can be referred to as *human factors and ergonomics* more generally speaking[1] (although I will mostly refer to it as "human factors" in this book). Ergonomics is composed of three main areas of research: physical ergonomics (e.g. physical fatigue while operating machines), cognitive ergonomics (e.g. understanding and remembering how a service works), and organizational ergonomics (e.g. optimization of processes). While the term ergonomics was only officially coined in 1950 from the Greek words *ergon* (work) and *nomos*

---

[1] Like the nonprofit organization Human Factors and Ergonomics Society (www.hfes.org).

DOI: 10.1201/9781003215370-4   23 (physical laws), there is evidence suggesting that ancient Greeks were actually applying ergonomics principles in their designs (Marmaras et al., 1999). For example, their amphitheaters were designed in a calculated effort to provide good visibility and acoustics from any seat in the audience, which demonstrates a concern for the experience of the end users. Any handle added to any pot in any civilization demonstrates a care for how its user is going to lift it and carry it around with more ease. In this sense, the UX mindset has been present since the beginning of humankind. The formalization of human factors principles, however, is much more recent.

Human factors is an applied science that started developing during the industrial revolution and was more firmly established during World War II, when lives were lost or expensive military equipment was destroyed because of human errors. In normal times, we can easily click or press the wrong button, so imagine the potential for error during wartime and under extreme stress … For instance, despite their heavy military training, pilots sometimes crashed their planes because they confused the landing gear with the flap handles. Regardless of intensive training, humans make errors. It's a fallacy to believe that humans can completely overcome their natural brain limitations; no matter how hard they try. You might have experienced this yourself during the SARS-Cov-2 pandemic, if you were trying very hard not to touch your face only to end up catching yourself doing so at some point. We're not good at controlling our impulses and paying attention to what we do all the time. Similarly, WW2 pilots were not the ones to blame. The issue came from a flaw in the design of the plane cockpits, more specifically the control configurations (e.g. Fitts and Jones, 1947) that did not account for human characteristics. The realization that certain designs could dramatically facilitate human error created a shift in mindsets. Instead of crafting machines in such a way to ease engineering and production costs, efforts started to be made to instead focus on accommodating those machines for human use. After all, saving on production costs and time doesn't matter if in the end the planes are short-lived because humans crash them. That's an important philosophy in UX: we care about investing on solutions that might be more inconvenient for the makers to put together in the short term (i.e. take more time, or be more costly to produce), but the return of investment in the long term is much greater because the product will last longer, won't be damaged by users, and, more importantly, won't hurt users. Psychologists thus started to be hired to account for human capabilities, performance, and limitations in the design of military equipment. After the war ended, this practice boomed in the workplace and for the development of consumer goods. Human factors science has a very close relationship with psychology and engineering (respectively *human factors psychology* and *human factors engineering*, which can often overlap) and can also have ties to computer science, architecture, education, or biology, among others.

Another notable moment in the history of UX is the work of Henry Dreyfuss, who is considered as the founding father of industrial design in the United States. For example, he redesigned the telephone in its "modern" appearance, which is still represented today in the telephone icon on our smartphones. In his book, *Designing for People*, originally published in 1955, he described his work as filling "the gaps between human behavior and machine design" (Dreyfuss, 2003, p. 34). "The most efficient machine," he explained, is "the one that is built around a person." Interestingly, he also describes his work like orchestrating a theater show. This sentiment was later echoed by designer (and game designer), researcher, and human-computer interaction (HCI) trailblazer Brenda Laurel. In her book *Computers as Theatre* (originally published in 1991), she explained that designing for specific human-computer experiences isn't about "building a better desktop." Rather, it's about "creating imaginary worlds that have a special relationship to reality: worlds in which we can extend, amplify, and enrich our own capacities to think, feel, and act" (Laurel, 2013, p. 40). This perspective paved the way to considering the emotional impact of technology, not only its functionality.

With the rise of personal computers in the 1980s, the HCI discipline emerged. Simply put, it's a branch of human factors that studies how humans interact with digital environments more specifically. HCI is at the intersection of psychology, cognitive and social sciences, technology, and computer science. With the explosion of technology in everyone's life in the past decades, human-centric practices became much more influential. One of the most well-known contributors in recent years is cognitive scientist and designer Donald Norman who championed HCD, a design process focusing on problem solving and accounting for human characteristics and needs. Another important cornerstone is the rise of *design thinking*, a creative process focusing on innovation that heavily relies on HCD. Design thinking has been most notably promoted by the famous design consultancy firm IDEO, founded by designer and engineer David Kelley in the early 1990s and behind the first usable mouse for Apple among many other innovations. In the 1990s, we also saw the rise and development of the concept of *usability*, most notably with the work of HCI researcher Jakob Nielsen. Simply put, usability is a quality attribute assessing the ease of use of a product or system; its *ability* to be *used*. Nielsen defined ten usability heuristics (Nielsen, 1994) to evaluate the quality of the interaction design of a system (which we will describe in Section 3.4).

Finally, the term UX was popularized by Don Norman in the 1990s when he named himself "user experience architect" at Apple. Norman realized that HCD wasn't accounting for all the different perceptions and interactions users are having with a product ecosystem (e.g. hearing about a product, buying it, contacting customer service), while they are still very important to their overall experience. *User experience* thus became an umbrella term considering the human factors for the entire user journey, although there is admittedly a lot of confusion around this term today (hence this book). Norman and Nielsen founded the NN Group firm (nngroup.com), today one of the leading UX research and consulting firms dedicated to improving people's experiences with technology.

There are countless and diverse researchers, practitioners, and advocates across the world who made UX (and overall human factors and HCI) what it is today. This short history was only a tiny slice of a rich cake to give you some perspective (albeit admittedly Western-centric) before diving in the science behind UX.

3.2 Human Factors and Cognitive Science

Human factors are sometimes referred to as "applied cognitive science" (for a comprehensive overview of human factors and ergonomics, see Stone et al., 2018). When you experience a product, a service, an environment, a game… it all happens in your brain, or more precisely, in your *mind*. Cognitive science is the scientific study of mental processes such as attention, memory, and reasoning allowing us to acquire knowledge, maintain and manipulate it, and overall make sense of the world. This is what the term *cognition* refers to. Cognitive science is the backbone of human factors and UX. It is sometimes confused with neuroscience (very trendy today!), which studies the nervous system and the biological basis of cognition. While neuroscience is fascinating and rapidly evolving, it isn't typically relevant or useful to UX work (at least not yet), despite what the "neurohype-surfers" would like you to believe. It might be one day, but for now the nervous system and its influence on our motivations, behaviors, and emotions, is still not well understood overall. So, no, you won't read about so-called "dopamine shots" and their hypothetical impact on our decision-making with an app in this book, I hope that's not too disappointing!

An experience is what happens in the mind, as a user perceives and interacts with a product. In order to create the best product possible for a human to use and enjoy, it's important to have at least a basic understanding of the capabilities, performance, and limitations of the mind. I'm going to give you a quick rundown (see Hodent, 2017, for a more detailed description of mental processes and application to video game development), so that you can have an overview of how our mental processes work (on average for neurotypical people). Figure 3.1 is an extremely simplified illustration of what is going on in the brain when we learn and process information (in reality, we do not have independent compartments dedicated to specific mental functions).

Information processing typically starts with the **perception** of what's going on around us (and inside of our body) and ends with a modification of our **memory**. The brain is constantly "re-wiring" itself depending on

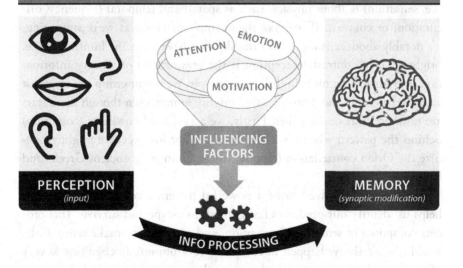

FIGURE 3.1
A simplified diagram of how the brain works. (From Hodent, C., *The Gamer's Brain: How Neuroscience and UX Can Impact Video Game Design*, CRC Press, Boca Raton, FL, 2017. With permission.)

what we experience in life. This is called *brain plasticity*, and we wouldn't be able to adapt to our ever-changing environment without it (for example, when we drastically had to adjust our way of living during the coronavirus pandemic). Between the perception of a stimulus and a change of memory, many biological, physiological, cognitive, and environmental factors are at play. Here, we will mainly talk about **attention**, which has a major impact on information processing and learning, and we will briefly explain the influence of **motivation** and **emotion**. Although I will describe these elements separately and in a certain order, keep in mind that they are not independent entities working serially one after the other to process information. Also, the brain does not *really* "process" information like a computer does. The brain is not a computer; it's an extremely complex living organ. The following is just a simplification of our main mental processes.

3.2.1 Perception

We do not perceive the world as it is. Perception is a construction of the mind, bound to be subjective. Humans do not perceive the world the way other animals do, or even other humans in many cases. It all starts with sensory information (i.e. stimuli) received by our receptor cells. While you might mostly be thinking of five specific senses (sight, hearing, touch, smell, and taste), we actually have many more. For example, we can sense our body in space (i.e. proprioception) and outside temperature. Sensory information (i.e. sensation) is about physics, such as spatial and temporal frequency, orientation, or contrast. If we take the example of vision as we're stargazing, it's notably about sensing dots in the sky that have a specific luminance (i.e. brightness). In contrast, perception is the *organization* of sensory information into something meaningful. For example, we might group the brightest stars together into the shape of, say, a mighty hunter, even though these stars are nowhere near one another. Lastly, we access the knowledge (cognition) behind the pattern when it's available to us. For instance, we might recognize the Orion constellation (represented as a hunter by ancient Greeks and Romans).

The brain has evolved to be a powerful pattern recognizer because this helps us identify our predators fast enough to escape and survive. This process composed of sensation, perception, and cognition to make sense of the world doesn't always happen in this order (bottom-up). Recognition is very often a top-down process, which means that our current knowledge about

FIGURE 3.2
Influence of context on perception. (From Hodent, C.,
The Gamer's Brain: How Neuroscience and UX Can
Impact Video Game Design, **CRC Press, Boca Raton,**
FL, 2017. With permission.)

FIGURE 3.2
Influence of context on perception. (From Hodent, C.,
The Gamer's Brain: How Neuroscience and UX Can
Impact Video Game Design, **CRC Press, Boca Raton,**
FL, 2017. With permission.)

the world (our cognition) influences our perception of it. For example, in Figure 3.2, you will perceive the stimulus at the center either as being a "B" or a "13" depending on the context and your expectation. Your knowledge of the world (cognition) is therefore influencing the way you perceive a specific stimulus.

This is why we commonly say that our senses are "tricking" us because we experience sensory illusions all the time, such as when we perceive depth on a flat (two-dimensional) screen, hear a different sound depending on what word we are currently reading, see colors differently than our neighbor (or even depending on our DNA in the case of color-blindness), or believe that our phone is vibrating in our pocket when it's actually on the table. Yet it's not our senses that are tricking us; it's our brains that are making it all up.

Perception is a subjective construction. As a result, all the stimuli that you create for your product (e.g. icons, copy, sound effects, visual effects, haptic feedback) won't necessarily be perceived by your users the way you intended. While certain HCI guidelines and principles can help anticipate how people will perceive and organize the visual and audio elements in your product up to a certain point (e.g. Gestalt principles of perception, described in Section 3.3), it will always be important to conduct UX tests to verify your assumptions. And since prior knowledge, expectation, context, and culture all influence perception, you will need to test your product with a diversity of users and situations, especially if your product is meant to be used across the world, and/or across generations. For example, a light bulb is not the symbol for "idea" for everyone. This perception actually depends on culture. Just like different cultures perceive something different in the stars making up the Orion constellation in Western culture. Similarly, the icon representing a floppy disk (still often used to express the saving functionality) won't necessarily be meaningful to young generations who have never interacted with this now retired object. You have your own subjective perception of the world; don't assume that others will necessarily have the same (i.e. egocentric bias).

3.2.2 Memory

Memory is the process of **encoding**, **storing**, and **retrieving** information. A popular model of memory suggests that it has three components: sensory memory, working (or short-term) memory, and long-term memory (Atkinson and Shiffrin, 1968), as shown in Figure 3.3. These are functional components instead of physical areas in the brain. **Sensory memory** is considered as being part of perception, and allows us to store information extremely briefly in a "sensory store." For example, persistence of vision, which allows us to see 24 images per second as an animated film, is due to sensory memory. We keep information in our sensory stores for a few hundred milliseconds, just in case we need to rapidly process this information (this might be a lion hidden in a bush!). If we do not pay attention to a particular element in our environment though, this information is usually lost in less than a second. If we actively pay attention to it, we start processing it in our working memory.

Working memory allows us to temporarily store *and* process information. This is where we "encode" information. For example, you are currently encoding information about working memory by temporarily storing words in your memory in order to make sense of them at the end of the sentence and (hopefully) learn something new about how information is encoded in your working memory (the longer the sentence, the harder it gets!). Working memory is extremely limited in time and space. You cannot store and process a lot of elements in working memory for too long. Imagine that you need to make a mental calculation, for example: 27×13. It can be challenging, yet you might be up for the challenge. Now, calculating 79×956 is typically very difficult for the untrained

FIGURE 3.3
Overview of memory. (From Hodent, C., *The Gamer's Brain: How Neuroscience and UX Can Impact Video Game Design*, CRC Press, Boca Raton, FL, 2017. With permission.)

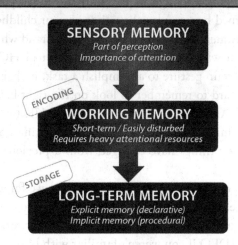

brain because it requires maintaining too many digits in mind while processing them. Furthermore, if something distracts you as you process this information (a notification on your phone, perhaps?) you're likely to lose track of your calculation. And then you need to start it all over again. Working memory requires a lot of attentional resources to function (our attentional resources are very scarce, as we will see in a moment) and is very easily distracted.

Once we're done processing information (after a few minutes maximum), it goes to long-term memory for storage. Do you remember the information about perception that you've likely encoded just minutes ago? It's already stored in your long-term memory. We have two main types of long-term memory: explicit memory and implicit memory. Explicit memory, also referred to as *declarative memory*, is storing all information and souvenirs that we can consciously retrieve and articulate (or "declare," hence its name). For example: your date of birth, what you ate for lunch yesterday, or what the definition of UX is. In contrast, implicit memory is more unconscious. One of the main forms of implicit memory is *procedural memory*, or more commonly named: muscle memory. It's the memory for actions: how to ride a bicycle, how to drive, draw, dance, play the piano, throw balls into hoops. It's also the memory for conditioning, such as when encoding multiplication tables by rote learning, or learning to fasten your seatbelt when your car emits a certain beep. Implicit memory is considered more robust (i.e. lasting longer) than explicit memory generally speaking, hence the common saying: "it's like riding a bike," although we certainly can forget procedural memories (if you've learned how to play the guitar in your childhood and haven't touched this instrument since, you probably understand what I mean). This is the main reason why conventions are important in HCI: when we are used to doing a certain gesture to accomplish a task, it's hard to learn a new one. Just like it's hard to remember to look on the right before crossing the street if you're an American freshly arrived in the UK (or vice versa). Old habits die hard. Similarly, a system update can sometimes be painful to get used to if too many things have changed from a previous version that we navigated well.

Overall, the main limitation of memory is that we forget a lot of information on average. Even if you carefully read the section about the history of UX just a few minutes ago, you might have already forgotten the name of the founder of IDEO if you weren't familiar with him (I apologize if you now feel compelled to go back a few pages to check!). Furthermore, what we do remember is not necessarily accurate. While perception is a construction of the brain, retrieving information in memory is a *reconstruction*. And every time we reconstruct a memory, we can potentially alter it (which opens the door to the hindsight bias described earlier), or even completely make it up! This happens every time we are sure that we did something, yet we did not. For example, you might wonder why your colleague hasn't yet completed the task you needed them to do and asked via email a few days ago. As you enquire when it will be done, your colleague asks: "What task are you talking about? You didn't send me any email." We can typically become annoyed as we're extremely confident about the fact that we did send that email, thus our colleague is either completely out of their mind or pulling our leg. Just to be sure, or maybe to demonstrate to your colleague that they are wrong, you double-check; only to realize that you did not in fact send that email. There might be a half-typed email in your draft folder, or maybe nothing at all. You *thought* of sending an email, yet did not, and your brain completely made up the memory of you sending the email. There's no need to panic if this happens to you once in a while; it's actually normal.

We cannot rely on our memory. That's the one thing to remember so that you can elaborate strategies to compensate. Highly trained pilots go through a detailed checklist before taking off; they know that memory is flawed. Safety protocols exist for a good reason. Take notes in meeting, send reminders, and establish to-do lists. Adjust your work and life environment to your brain limitations. As for the product that you may be building, it's important not to assume that users will remember something they have learned in a tutorial, or even an action that they just did. Do not rely on users' memory, or yours; it's fallible. Adjust the environment instead.

3.2.3 Attention

Attention is about selecting what elements in our environment to process, and what to ignore. It's the resource we need to process information in working memory, so to speak. Attention can be active (i.e. top-down) when we decide to pay attention to something in particular, such as reading this book. Or it can be passive (i.e. bottom-up) when something from the environment "grabs" your attention, such as if you receive a text message while reading this book. Attention can be selective (focused on one element), or divided (what we commonly call "multitasking"). In any case, it's best described as working like a filter: when you focus your attention on something, you filter out the rest. Which means that you do not carefully process the numerous stimuli assailing your senses continuously. To the point that a big change can sometimes go completely unnoticed, such as the brand new haircut of our partner. And no, women are not better than men on average at paying attention to details or at multitasking, and technology is not reducing our attention span. Human attention has never been good. Try singing a song with English lyrics while underlining or highlighting the verbs in the next paragraph; you will experience how scarce our attentional resources are.

Many accidents happen because humans did not pay attention to a warning signal, lost concentration on their task, or got completely distracted. Yet again, we're pretty confident that we can do several things at the same time. But it can only be true if those tasks do not require much attention to complete, such as automated tasks like chewing gum and walking. This is why well-contrasting buttons on a website (i.e. a "call to action") are needed to draw attention to the functionalities that we assume are the most important for users. When we need to attend too many things at the same time, we experience "cognitive load" and it can be draining. The first days at a new job can feel this way because many things are new and need to be learned (i.e. processed in working memory). A user discovering a new app can similarly feel overwhelmed if there are too many new things to process, which is why we try to reduce the cognitive load overall by *onboarding* a new user progressively, and direct their attention to what we assume matters the most to them (which we verify). Attention is a finite and very limited resource that needs to be carefully handled.

3.2.4 Motivation

If we're not motivated to do something, we don't do it. Picking up the phone, cooking dinner, using an application, working with a tool, browsing a website ... all of these actions require motivation to be accomplished. While we don't yet have a unified theory of motivation that can explain all of our behaviors, we have a broad idea of the different types of motivation. They can be grouped into four main categories: implicit motivation (i.e. biological drives, such as wanting to go to bed because our brain produces melatonin at night, a hormone that promotes sleep), individual needs (i.e. what we care about depending on our personality), extrinsic motivation (i.e. what we do in order to gain something external to the task), and intrinsic motivation (i.e. engaging in an activity for its own sake). Contrary to popular belief, those different types of motivation don't have a specific hierarchy. The well-known Maslow's theory of motivation (elaborated in the 1940s) stating that humans fulfill needs in a certain priority (e.g. physiological needs such as food will be satisfied in priority over "higher" needs such as love and belonging) is actually greatly criticized today because of its hierarchical construction. Despite its flaws, Maslow's theory is still very popular, although probably not as much as the highly controversial Myers-Briggs personality test. Also known as MBTI, this test is widely used today for recruitment and team management despite not having any scientific evidence of its validity (see for example Pittenger, 1993).

This is the main issue with human motivation: everyone wants to understand how it works but since science doesn't have clear and universal answers, it's opening the door to all kinds of quacks, from people claiming that "dopamine shots" rule your mind to people practicing the equivalent of Tarot reading wrapped in a pseudo-scientific tool to look more serious. Be very careful about extraordinary claims regarding the brain and the mind in general, and more specifically when it relates to motivation. Especially when it comes to implicit motivation (biological drives) and individual needs (personality), whose impact on our behavior isn't well understood at all. We do not yet precisely understand how hormones impact our feelings and behavior (and we may never will, as it's extremely complex), and most personality tests that are available aren't valid scientifically (therefore aren't useful, other than to just have fun with them). So far, the most robust model of personality that we have is the "Big Five" personality traits, also known as OCEAN, with five factors shaping our personality: Openness to experience (how curious we are), Conscientiousness (how organized we are), Extraversion (how outgoing we are), Agreeableness (how compassionate we are), and Neuroticism (how sensitive and nervous we are). Yet, even this robust model doesn't explain all of human personality, and it cannot accurately predict behavior based on someone's OCEAN results.

It's not an easy task to understand, and even more so anticipate, how the different types of motivations will influence our perception, cognition, feelings, and behavior. I will here focus on what we currently understand best: extrinsic motivation and intrinsic motivation. Extrinsic motivation relates to how our interaction with the environment shapes our behavior. It's the carrots and sticks of motivation (i.e. conditioning or behavioral psychology). Simply put, we are generally more motivated to repeat a behavior that previously led to a reward (i.e. something pleasant) while we will usually avoid repeating a behavior that led to a punishment (i.e. something annoying, painful, or even the absence of a reward). We learn a lot through conditioning: our multiplication tables, which food makes us sick and we should avoid, that we should fasten our seatbelt if we want the annoying beep to stop, that we should verify that the bottle of juice is tightly closed before shaking it, that having a job will provide us with money, and so on.

While extrinsic motivation is certainly important, it does not account for all human behavior: we often do an activity just for the sake of it, not to gain any external rewards or avoid punishments. Hopefully, you're currently reading these lines not because you have to for your job or to please someone, but because you are intrinsically interested in understanding the brain. Playing is another activity that is typically intrinsically motivating, unless you are paid to play games or you play to please someone else. The most robust framework addressing intrinsic motivation is the *self-determination theory* (SDT). It posits that the activities that are intrinsically motivating are the ones satisfying our needs for competence, autonomy, and relatedness (Ryan and Deci, 2000). **Competence** is about feeling a sense of progression and feeling in control. For example, if you start a new activity (e.g. yoga, painting, playing a music instrument) and you feel that you're progressing as you practice, it's satisfying and it will encourage you to keep going. If we don't have a sense of increasing mastery, or if our progress is not perceptible, then we're more likely to drop the activity. At work, it's motivating to be promoted because climbing up the ladder generally means that we're getting better at our job (or at least that's the common perception). **Autonomy** relates to the feeling of self-expression (e.g. being creative) and of having meaningful choices. For example, it's usually more satisfying to be given an objective at work and have *carte blanche* to reach it than being micro-managed by our boss. Last but not least, humans are an incredibly social species (we need each other to survive!); **relatedness** is thus a powerful need. Activities when we cooperate with others in a meaningful way, such as when everyone has a specific role, is satisfying. But even simply hanging out and sharing good times with people we like is motivating.

There are still many things that we don't understand about motivation, but this simplified breakdown into implicit motivation, personality, extrinsic motivation, and intrinsic motivation gives you a broad overview. Motivation has an important impact on attention on memory: we typically process and retain information that we care about better than non-meaningful information.

3.2.5 Emotion

Emotion refers to a state of physiological arousal (such as an accelerating heart rate), as well as a feeling associated with it when applicable (e.g. fear). Although emotions and how they work are complex and still mysterious in many ways, we generally consider the limbic system as being the main system involved with emotional responses. This system identifies the situation in terms of survival (e.g. are we in present danger?), based on what is stored in memory, and regulates the production of hormones accordingly. For example, in the presence of a potential predator, adrenaline and cortisol are produced to raise awareness and tense muscles to ready the fight or flight response. The new event will then be stored in memory in order to make us even more responsive next time.

Generally speaking, emotion helps us reason and survive. But it can also influence us into making irrational decisions. We have countless biases impacting our everyday life, and many of them are influenced by emotion. For example, *loss aversion* is a phenomenon whereby a loss triggers a more powerful emotional response than an equivalent gain. Our pain of losing is more intense than our joy of gaining. This can for example make us susceptible to the "sunk-cost fallacy" that make us hold on to something that is losing value (such as a stock crashing) because the pain of selling it at a loss is too strong, and as a result can make us lose even more money as we wait too long in the hope that the stock value will increase again. Emotion is thus impacting our cognition. On the other hand, cognition can also impact our emotion. For example, we typically appreciate a meal better if it's presented elegantly, and if you like champagne you might gain more pleasure from an expensive and reputable brand. Aesthetics and heightened expectations have a positive impact on appreciation (as long as those expectations are not later betrayed). Emotion and cognition interact with one another in many ways.

3.2.6 To summarize: main limitations of our mental processes

Perception is subjective, memory is fallible, and attentional resources are scarce. Not only do we have quite important limitations of our mental processes but we also are mostly unaware of them. Sometimes blissfully (it allows us to feel good about our capabilities), sometimes catastrophically when it results in a fatal error. From the sinking of the Titanic, to the Chernobyl disaster, to the spread of a virus by omission of hygiene rules, to everyday incidents and accidents, human neglect and errors are everywhere (see Reason, 2013, for a deeper dive in the varieties of human error).

Motivation and emotion have a complex impact on our mental processes, and our cognition (i.e. our prior knowledge and expectation) can even have an impact on our emotion. In his seminal book *Thinking, Fast and Slow* (2011), professor in psychology and Nobel laureate Daniel Kahneman explains that the brain has two main modes of thinking, which he calls *System 1* and *System 2*. System 1 is fast, automatic, and effortless, and it allows us to make most of the countless decisions we need to make all day long. It's the system for routines, automatic behavior such as driving a car on a familiar and empty road (if you're already an experienced driver), or knowing that three times six equals eighteen (if you've learned your multiplication tables by heart in English). And it's the system for conditioned response such as buckling your seatbelt when you hear a beep, or fight-or-flight response. In comparison, System 2 is consuming more energy and attentional resources. It allows us to make complex calculations and effortful reasoning. To simplify, System 1 is our intuitive thinking while System 2 is where rational thinking lies. System 1 is very efficient but it's also very biased and doesn't turn off to let

System 2 completely take over when a complex task needs solving. This is why the human brain, despite its great performance and capability, often falls into traps and makes mistakes. We are not the rational beings that we believe we are. In fact, our irrational thinking is so systemic that it is predictable, as behavioral psychologist Dan Ariely explains in his very approachable and insightful book *Predictably Irrational* (2008).

If we care to offer the best experience possible to humans, we cannot just account for brain capabilities; we must also and mostly account for its numerous limitations and biases. Make no mistake; your users will make errors as they use your product and service. And you will make irrational decisions during the development cycle if you don't have a good process and methodologies to avoid them (such as relying on a rigorous scientific approach to identify problems and find out where they are coming from). Anticipating and accounting for these errors (both on the creators' and the users' sides) are entirely part of the product development work and are core to the UX mindset.

3.3 HCI Principles

Now that you have a high-level understanding of the characteristics of the brain and its limitations, let's talk about the HCI principles accounting for them. While this book is not about diving into HCI principles, it can still be interesting to at least be familiar with a few of the most well-known notions. Here's a quick rundown.

3.3.1 *Gestalt principles of perception*

As we saw earlier, perception is subjective. However, we have general laws that can predict how certain stimuli will be perceived by humans overall; the Gestalt principles. Developed by German psychologists in the 1920s (see Wertheimer, 1923), these principles account for how the human mind organizes the environment. For example, the law of similarity states that elements that have the same attribute (e.g. color, shape, size, brightness, pitch, tone duration, softness, temperature) will be perceived as belonging together. This is how we perceive the brightest stars in our skies as belonging to a constellation. In Figure 3.4, you perceive lines of circles and squares on the top left, while you perceive columns on the top right. We group together and perceive specific patterns depending on the attributes

FIGURE 3.4
Gestalt's law of similarity (top) and proximity (bottom).

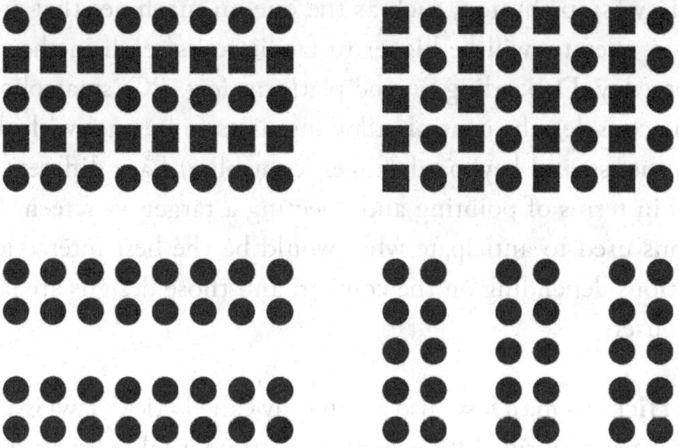

of the stimuli. Another example is the law of proximity; we group together elements that are close to one another. This is why you perceive lines on the bottom left of Figure 3.4 while you perceive columns on the bottom right. Having less space (i.e. padding) between an image and its caption than between the caption and the next paragraph is helping readers understand the hierarchy of the interface; which text goes with what. Several other Gestalt laws exist and, when they are violated, they make it harder for users to make sense of how a system or an interface is organized and works. In the book *Designing With the Mind in Mind*, Jeff Johnson (2010) provides a lot of examples of how to use Gestalt laws to improve interface design.

3.3.2 Fitts's law, Hick-Hyman law, Pareto principle, and Von Restorff effect

- **Fitts's law** is probably the most well-known HCI law. It's a predictive model of motor behavior. More specifically, it predicts the time it will take a human to point at an element (such as using a mouse to point at an icon on a graphical user interface—GUI, or reaching a button with a finger). This model allows anticipating how big a button should be and where it should be placed to facilitate its targeting and avoid errors such as clicking on the wrong button. It guides interaction designers in defining what is the best way for users to interact with a system. For example, a "cancel" button might be designed smaller to avoid users accidentally clicking on it and thus interrupting a downloading process, especially when this process is long. On the contrary, a safety "stop" button, such as the one on machines that are dangerous to operate, will be bigger to facilitate its reach in the case of an emergency. Depending on the platform (e.g. PC, smartphone, video game console), the controls allowing users to interact with the system (e.g. mouse and keyboard, finger, controller) have different pros and cons in terms of pointing and selecting a target on screen. Fitts's law is thus used to anticipate what would be the best interaction design solutions depending on the context, and those designs are later tested with users.

- **The Hick-Hyman law** (also commonly called Hick's law) is a model for choice reaction time. It posits that the time it takes for a user to make a decision will logarithmically increase with the number of options displayed. This is the main reason why it's usually recommended to narrow down options for users, especially on a home screen. The more options, the more time it takes us to make a decision, and we eventually might decide to just disengage with the product or service altogether. The brain has a tendency to take the path of least resistance, and oftentimes deciding to not decide is easier than finding the right option for us (this is a bias called the status quo bias or default bias). If your system has many options to choose from (e.g. a website to buy a train ticket, or browse the real estate marketplace), filtering and sorting functionalities allow narrowing these options down according to users' goals and situation. For example, when browsing for real estate, it's much less overwhelming to narrow down options within the price range that we can afford and with many different filtering options (e.g. home type, number of bedrooms, location).

- **The Pareto principle**, also known as the "80/20 rule," posits that 20% of the variables in a system are responsible for 80% of the results. For example, 80% of your users' interaction with your system will concern only 20% of the system features. It's important to define what are the main features that will be useful for most of your users and to place those features in the forefront. Defining the most commonly used features will also help you avoid the choice overload (or "analysis paralysis") illustrated with Hick's law. Google search engine is a striking example of this: the google.com landing page is very simple and emphasizes the field where users can type what they are searching for. There is no fluff or distraction, helping users accomplish their goals. Define what your product is essentially about and why would users primarily use it, and avoid getting lost with a plethora of options that would unnecessarily complicate your home screen.

- **The Von Restorff effect** is quite simple to explain: the more an element stands out from its surroundings, the better we remember it. This is tied to what is called *perceptual salience*: Our attentional resources are scarce, so it can be difficult for us to isolate an immobile lioness hiding in tall yellow grass, or the voice of someone we know among the cacophony of a cocktail party. It's much easier for us to spot and therefore process in working memory an object that contrasts well with the rest, such as a moving object among still objects, a bright object among dull objects, a louder noise, or a brighter light. The salience bias and the Von Restorff effect allow designers to carefully select where to draw attention, depending on what makes sense for users. If too many elements are trying to draw attention in an interface, then nothing *really* stands out.

3.3.3 Mental models

Mental models are a critical concept in UX because it's about acknowledging that users have a certain mental representation (i.e. conceptual model) of how a system works depending on their prior knowledge and understanding of the system, and which might differ from the mental model of the creators of said system (i.e. their conceptualization and representation of the envisioned system). In his seminal book *The Design of Everyday Things* (2013), Donald Norman explains how users' mental model of a system might make them use it wrongly. Norman takes the example of a thermostat. Let's say that you're usually comfortable in a room at around 20°C (roughly 68°F). You arrive in a hotel room in the middle of winter and you're frozen to the bones. The thermostat tells you that the room is currently at 14°C (57°F), so you decide to crank it up to 25°C (77°F) in the hope that the room will warm up faster. Except that it won't. The room will reach your desired temperature of 20°C at the same time whether you set it up to 20°C or 25°C. Just like an oven, the heating system is on/off; it's not gradual. To stay at the desired temperature, it turns on and off alternatively. That's how this system is built. But it's typically not the mental model that we have. Users can have a very different mental model of how things work, and it can oftentimes lead to errors. Interaction designers need to consider what mental model their users have, so that they can adequately communicate to users how a system works.

Another example that can commonly bring confusion to web surfers is which page we will land on if we click on the "back" button (typically represented by an arrow pointing left). Let's say that you're browsing Wikipedia. You start on the "user experience" page (let's call it page A) and from here you click on the word "usability" which leads you to another page (page B). From this page, you click on the phrase "human-computer interaction" to learn more about this field (page C). After gaining the information you wanted from page C, you click on the back button, which brings you to page B. But then, you want to double-check something on the "human-computer interaction" page (page C), which is the page you were right before going back to page B. Will clicking on the back button bring you to the just previously visited web page C? Some people believe so, except that clicking back will bring you to page A instead. What may seem obvious to the people who built a system, or who are very savvy in using a system, might be completely illogical to others.

As a creator or someone very familiar with an environment, you have a strong bias called "the curse of knowledge." If you've ever asked for directions in an unfamiliar neighborhood to someone who's been living there for several years, you might have had difficulty following the directions, although it seemed very obvious to the person giving them to you. Just like perception, mental models are subjective and highly dependent on our prior knowledge. Having a UX mindset is about understanding and considering the different mental models your users have.

3.3.4 Affordance

One last very important concept in interaction design is "affordance." An affordance is the "relationship between the properties of an object and the capabilities of the agent that determine just how the object could possibly be used" (Norman, 2013). Simply put, there's an affordance when the characteristics of an object facilitate your interaction with it. Take the example of a mug: if it has a well-designed handle, it allows most users to lift the mug with only three fingers and without burning themselves when the mug is filled with a hot beverage. A handle on a door *affords* you to grab it and

FIGURE 3.5
A frustrating experience with a door presenting a false affordance. (Illustration by Laura Taylor.)

pull the door open. And just by looking at the door you might form expectations about how to open it since the handle makes you anticipate that it probably needs to be pulled (unless the door is badly designed and it needs to be pushed contrary to our expectation—and no, most people won't read the label "PUSH," as illustrated in Figure 3.5). This knowledge (or mental model) of how to use objects with handles is the perceivable part of an affordance, which Don Norman calls a "signifier." In architecture and industrial design, a similar concept to affordance is the "form follows function" principle, which is mainly about carefully designing the shape of a building or object in relation to its functionality.

According to researcher and UX expert Rex Hartson (2003), there are four kinds of affordances:

- **Physical affordances**: the physical attributes of an object that facilitate its manipulation (e.g. the handle on the mug, or the holes in a bowling ball). Fitts's law, which we've explained earlier, is about improving the physical affordance of an object or interface.
- **Cognitive affordances (i.e. signifiers)**: the shapes, labels, metaphors that convey the functionality of an element, and how to use it. For example, the icon representing an envelope helps users understand that this functionality is about sending a message (assuming

that users have the appropriate mental model associated with this metaphor).

- **Sensory affordances**: features helping users to sense something, such as using a large font to ensure that everyone can read it.
- **Functional affordances**: features allowing users to accomplish certain tasks more efficiently, such as comparison, filtering, or sorting features.

As these few examples illustrate, HCI guidelines and principles are all about understanding how humans think and interact with their environment. Good design is about understanding and adjusting for human capabilities, performance, and limitations.

3.4 Usability Heuristics

Usability is what we aim for in HCI: making a product easy to use (i.e. effective), efficient, and satisfying for all users as they interact with it in various situations (see Nielsen, 2012). Usability is about minding the brain limitations in terms of perception, memory, and attention, thus the need for basic knowledge in cognitive science. Evaluating the usability of a product or service is about anticipating (with specific guidelines) and later verifying (via usability testing) if it's easy and satisfying to use. It's about chasing down all the frustrations that users might experience, understanding why they are happening, and fixing them within the production constraints. It's also about prioritizing what issues absolutely need to be fixed first. This evaluation is conducted by using usability heuristics.

A heuristic is a rule of thumb, a mental shortcut, or in this case, a broad design principle. The most popular usability heuristics are the ones established by Jakob Nielsen (1994). The first heuristic of his list is called "visibility of system status." It emphasizes that a system should always keep the user informed about what is going on. If you click on a button to buy an item on a shopping website, then you should immediately see clear feedback telling you that this item is added to your cart. Then, you should understand how to check out or how to keep shopping, depending on your current goal. Designers who care about UX do not conceal controls, they instead make sure to convey how something is supposed to be operated (Dreyfuss, 2003). Users should always understand what they can do with the system, what is currently going on, and what has just happened (i.e. the system should be "transparent").

Nielsen's ten usability heuristics are described below.[2]

1. **Visibility of system status**: The system should convey information to users regarding what actions can be done and give fast and appropriate feedback upon users' action.

2. **Match between the system and the real world**: The system should communicate using familiar concepts for the target audience and use metaphors or analogies to the real world (e.g. "folders" in an interface match a real-world concept).

3. **User control and freedom**: Users should be able to make mistakes or change their mind.

4. **Consistency and standards**: It's important to follow platform and industry conventions so that users can already be familiar with how the system works.

5. **Error prevention**: The system should be designed in a way to prevent user errors from occurring (e.g. a confirmation screen preventing you from closing a tool before saving your work).

6. **Recognition rather than recall**: To minimize a user's memory load, it's important to make objects, actions, and options visible. Avoid forcing the user to remember information.

7. **Flexibility and efficiency of use**: Offer users the possibility to tailor their experience with customizable options.

8. **Aesthetic and minimalist design**: Remove all irrelevant and distracting information.

9. **Error recovery**: Help users recognize, diagnose, and recover from errors.

10. **Help and documentation**: Even though a system should be usable without documentation, it is important to offer users efficient and intelligible help when they need it.

If you want to learn more about usability, I would recommend the popular and very approachable book *Don't Make Me Think* by usability expert Steve Krug (2014), which provides a lot of practical examples on how to make your web pages and apps more usable. However, avoid considering usability as "common sense," despite what the subtitle of Krug's book suggests

---

[2]https://www.nngroup.com/articles/ten-usability-heuristics/.

(i.e. *A Common Sense Approach to Web Usability*). As we saw earlier, common sense is only as good as your current understanding on a subject. Your own perception of your product and your users is subjective, and can potentially be very biased. The whole point of adopting a UX mindset and practices is to avoid relying on your personal gut feelings and to instead shift into adopting the perspective of your users (who, by the way, don't care about your feelings, they just want to get something done as seamlessly as possible). Usability guidelines allow you to identify, understand, and fix the friction points that your users might encounter as they are trying to accomplish their goals with your product. Memory is fallible and attentional resources are scarce not just for users, but for product creators as well, so follow usability guidelines to avoid falling right back into your biased gut feelings.

3.5 Emotional Design and Engagement

While ease of use is certainly important, it's not everything in the experience of a product. As we mentioned earlier, the aesthetic quality of an object can alter our appreciation of it. It's not just the cooking that makes the delicious meal; it's also its presentation. Similarly the aesthetics quality of your product or environment will have an impact on users' experience. In fact, the Aesthetic-Usability effect in HCI posits that users can tolerate minor usability issues when an interface is visually appealing (but look and feel cannot save you from critical usability issues). Humans are more attracted to an aesthetically pleasing object over a neutral one, even when the latter has more features. Take the example of the first iPhone that managed to take over then smartphone leader BlackBerry. Even though the iPhone had far fewer features when it first launched, it was found "sexier" than the BlackBerry and it quickly became the new leader on the market. Many elements beyond aesthetics impact the emotions we feel as we interact with a product. Narrative design is another example: it's much more pleasurable to use tools that greet us (e.g. the Apple Mac saying "Hello" on first boot) and communicate with us like other human beings would, especially when errors occur (e.g. the "error 404" message, when a server cannot find the requested web page, is not particularly endearing).

Usability is not everything. Sure, we use tools to accomplish goals, but emotional design is also important. According to Donald Norman (2005), any design has three levels of processing: visceral, behavioral, and reflective, which interlace emotion and cognition. The visceral level triggers automatic emotional responses. It's the feeling of attraction or repulsion for an object; it's about appearances. The behavioral level has to do with the function, performance, and usability of an object. Finally, the reflective level is about the intellectualization of a product, such as the message and values it conveys, the self-image reflected by using it, or the memories it triggers. Take a jacket. The visceral level is concerned about how it looks and how it feels: the cut, the color, and the softness of the fabric. You might love it or hate it at first sight or touch. At the behavioral level, the concern will be more about if it's easy to put on, if it's practical to wash, or if it has enough pockets. The reflective level would be, for example, how it was made. If you recognize the brand as one that treats their employees poorly and damages the environment, you might be uncomfortable buying the jacket because it doesn't align with your values. Design, says Norman, must take place at all these levels. Thus, do not neglect the emotional design of your products, even if they are utilitarian tools.

Some products need to have an even greater focus on emotion, such as video games. Art forms and entertainment systems cannot just be usable; they must also elicit emotions. Interactive entertainment is not a means to an end. Video games, movie theaters, or amusement parks must be fun, otherwise there's absolutely no reason to interact with those systems. A game typically needs to pique our curiosity and challenge our skills. It would certainly be more usable to only have to click on one button to win a game, but that's not fun. The problem is, what *is* fun? While we don't currently have established models in HCI to break down fun, I proposed the notion of "engage-ability" (Hodent, 2017) from my experience in game UX (video game development more specifically). We might not all agree about what fun is, but when we are having fun it means that we are *engaged* with the system. I describe engage-ability as being composed of three main pillars: motivation (both extrinsic and intrinsic), emotion (pleasure of use and discovery), and game flow (level of challenge and learning curve).

Making a system more engaging is critical for entertainment, but it can also be important for education systems or health applications, and it revolves a lot around making users (or players) feel a sense of competence, autonomy, and relatedness (see the description of SDT earlier). *Gamification* is popular, and it can provide an interesting perspective as long as the idea is not merely to consider extrinsic rewards (i.e. simply adding badges when users accomplish tasks). This is why I prefer to use the term *playful learning*. If the objective is *really* to add fun to an educational system and to focus on learners' engagement then you must also consider fostering intrinsic motivation by learning through play.

We must always start by asking ourselves *why* would users want to be engaged with a product or system. People don't want to be engaged with the social media platform they use *per se*, they care about being engaged with other people (i.e. relatedness). And they certainly don't want to be engaged with a basic tool such as a scheduling system; they will actually be more satisfied if they spend the least amount of time necessary using the tool to schedule meetings. While the three levels of emotional design are always important to consider, engage-ability is not always a useful framework. It depends on your product and what problems you are trying to solve for your users (simplifying their lives or entertaining them). As always in UX, we first care about users' needs, wants, and best interests.

4

The Process and
Methodologies of UX

While knowledge in cognitive science and application of HCI principles are essential ingredients for a UX mindset, they do not constitute a recipe for good experience by themselves. Human-centered design (HCD) is fundamentally an *iterative* process with users at its core. It doesn't matter how experienced UX experts are, they are not going to get a design right on their first trial. HCI guidelines offer a good starting point and will allow them to avoid common pitfalls, but it's not going to make their design good. The end product is also not going to provide a great experience if end users were not entirely part of the design process. Having time to iterate with users is thus key to UX. Iteration is a powerful tool to uncover what we do not yet understand and to find the right solutions for users.

The iterative loop consists of first understanding users and what problems we need to solve for them, generating ideas, prototyping, and then testing the design with users. After a few iterations, once the design is refined, it can be then implemented and tested again before and after its release to the world to fine-tune it (depending on your product, these steps can vary a little bit). This iterative process allows failure early and often, and the ability to learn from these failures in order to improve the product in development, at a time when it's cheaper to fail and easier to fix issues. In this chapter, we're going to tour the UX design process and explain a few methodologies along the way.

DOI: 10.1201/9781003215370-5

4.1 Design Thinking

Design thinking is a HCD approach that focuses on innovation. There's sometimes a misconception that UX practices cannot lead to innovation, often backed up by a popular quote attributed (possibly falsely) to Henry Ford: "If I had asked people what they wanted, they would have said faster horses." We don't ask users to tell us what we should design for them, we instead observe them interact with their environment, we ask them what frustrations they encounter, we identify the origin of their problems, we brainstorm multiple ideas, and we create numerous prototypes which we test with users to see what fails and what is promising. If your new ideas and inventions don't meet a market, don't satisfy a need, and are not implemented well, then they won't become innovations having the potential to change people's lives. The design thinking framework typically consists of three main stages (Gibbons, 2016), as illustrated in Figure 4.1:

1. understand users (empathize) and define what their problems are,
2. explore by generating ideas and prototyping,
3. materialize by testing your prototypes, iterating, and later on implementing.

These stages can be repeated and can each influence another, instead of being strictly linear.

The renowned design firm IDEO has been championing design thinking for decades, from designing the first Apple mouse to designing the ingenious first wearable breast pump (Willow), or the impactful prescription home delivery and organizer system (PillPack). They have three overlapping criteria for innovation, according to industrial designer and IDEO chair Tim Brown (2019):

- feasibility (what's functionally possible within the material and time constraints),
- viability (sustainable business model),
- desirability (what makes sense to people and for people).

There can be no innovation without considering the feasibility, viability, *and* desirability of an invention. Furthermore, desirability entails a care and empathy for people (the future users of a product). "New opportunities for innovation open up when you start the creative problem-solving process with empathy toward your target audience," as IDEO founder David Kelley and his brother

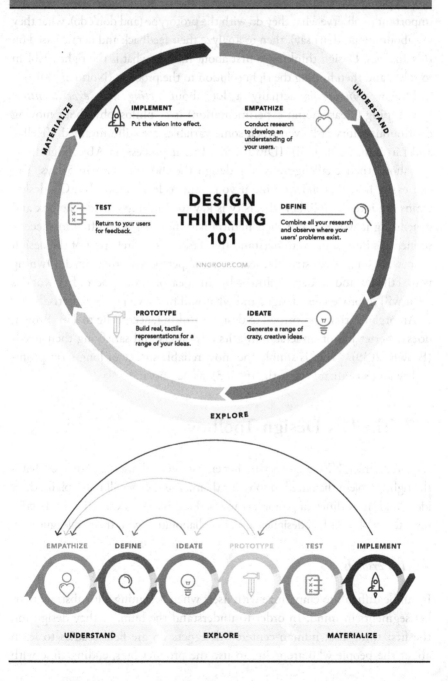

FIGURE 4.1
Design thinking process by Sarah Gibbons
(nngroup.com).

and partner Tom Kelley explain (Kelley and Kelley, 2013, p. 17). With empathy and a will to solve people's problems in mind, the key is then to explore various ideas without getting too attached to any specific one. Quick and dirty prototypes are created to test these ideas with end users and stakeholders. It's important to observe what they do with the prototype (and don't do), what they say about it (and don't say), then to analyze their feedback and iterate based on this analysis. Design thinking is first about finding what is the right problem to solve, and then finding the right solution to the problem (Norman, 2013).

Design *thinking* is actually a lot about *acting* and *experimenting*. Prototyping (ideation and experimentation) is a "philosophy about moving continuously forward, even when some variables are still unrefined" (Kelley and Littman, 2001, p. 4). IDEO showed their process on ABC Nightline's TV show: their challenge was to redesign the shopping cart in 5 days. You can easily find this show online if you want to learn more. IDEO's design teams are interdisciplinary (diversity is key to thinking outside the box and generating new ideas) and their mantra is to fail early and often to succeed sooner. It's important to understand that failure is entirely part of the design process, as long as constructive learning and perspective are gained. Owning your failures and understanding why an idea or prototype didn't work is what will improve your design, and what will make you gain expertise.

An organization committed to design thinking, according to Tim Brown, does a better job of understanding its customers and satisfying their needs (Brown, 2019). "That is simply the most reliable source of long-term profitability and sustainable growth" (p. 183), as he puts it.

4.2 The UX Design Toolbox

As stated earlier, UX designers will first empathize with users and define what is the right problem they need to solve for them. Then, they will make plans, draft ideas, and create different prototypes to test. Here is a non-exhaustive list describing a few tools that UX designers use, in collaboration with their colleagues.

4.2.1 Personas

It can be difficult to empathize with users when designing with abstract market segments in mind. In order to understand the humans they design for, the first thing that human-centered designers do are field studies to learn about the people who are going to use the product by spending time with them in their natural environment, observing how they work, discussing with them, identifying what they might need and what their goals are. It's about finding out what they like about their job (or the activity that the product will be a part of), what they don't like, what frictions they encounter, and the problems that you can solve for them. A field study will provide you with a ton of insights that cannot be summarized in a spreadsheet. The persona method is about distilling all of these insights from real people into a profile with specific goals, desires, expectations, routines, and even a specific name and photo, so that it can be used to support the design thinking process. It's about shifting from being data-driven to being *insights*-driven, and shifting the design focus from users' tasks (e.g. reading a recipe online) to users' *goals* (e.g. cooking, which now considers when, where, and how the user will read the recipe, and what they are likely doing at the same time). According to designer and programmer Alan Cooper who coined the term and popularized the method, personas are "*hypothetical archetypes* of actual users" (Cooper, 2004, p. 122). While we might lose track of the fact that "users" are real people with feelings and emotions, personas allow referring to specific individuals. As Cooper puts it, "Designing for a *single user* is the most effective way to satisfy a broad population" (p. 125), and it avoids the development team thinking of themselves as the user. Designer Kim Goodwin explains in detail what personas are, how to create them properly, and how to use them efficiently in her book *Designing for the Digital Age* (2009). She states that personas are "composite models of user behavior patterns" that were observed and analyzed from all the data gathered during the preliminary research (i.e. field study). "Personas will help you determine what that data means, convey that meaning to product team members in a compelling and memorable way, make better design decisions, and build consensus around a direction" (p. 229). Thus, personas will be very useful for design and marketing teams, as well as to communicate across teams and with stakeholders.

Personas are defined by a type of user's goals. For example, if you're creating an educational platform that will be used by teachers, students, and parents, each of these user types will have different goals. One persona is defined per goal. The most important personas are the *primary personas*: the individuals who are the main focus of the design. According to Cooper, each primary persona requires a unique interface. In our example, the teacher should have a different interface than the student or the parent, which means that in this case, three interfaces should be designed for this platform. If you end up with too many primary personas, your intended product might be too broad, too costly to build properly to cater everyone's needs, and end up satisfying no one. Carefully defining primary personas will help you prioritize and narrow down whom your product is for.

The persona method is a great tool for empathy, team alignment (especially the process of creating persona), and prioritization. It has its vulnerabilities though, such as the risk of falling into stereotypes, which can sometimes end up being harmful to some of your users (and your product, consequently). Having a diverse and inclusive team, and conducting your UX research with a diverse representation of users will help you avoid this caveat. It's also critical to create personas based on reliable and regularly updated data reflecting your real target audience for the product you are currently developing. This is why personas should not be re-used from one product to the next. It's a tool to keep yourself connected with the humans behind market segmentation; therefore, recycling personas will entirely defeat the purpose, not to mention that it's the *process* of creating personas that provides the insights you need.

4.2.2 *Content strategy and elements of UX*

Content strategy is mostly about balancing business goals and production constraints (product objectives) with users' needs. People don't want features; they want to accomplish certain goals. As Donald Norman says, people don't want a drill; they *need* to make holes. But what they *really want* is to install bookshelves (Norman, 2013). Focus on what is *really* meaningful to your target audience, what will solve their problems and improve their lives. Before defining all of what your product or system should do, start by asking yourself *why* adding a certain feature would matter to people, and to accomplish what goals. The risk is always to add too many features that are not *really* relevant to actual users, and to end up with a product that lacks clarity and is too complex to use. Again, the important thing is to figure out what experience your users will have, more than what features to add. As UX designer Jesse James Garrett puts it, "Features and functions always matter, but user experience has a far greater effect on customer loyalty" (Garrett, 2011). Having an overall idea of your content strategy from the perspective of your target user needs to happen *before* you start defining the features and architecture of your product, and should be refined all throughout the product development cycle.

In his book *The Elements of User Experience* (2011), Garrett explains his popular conceptual framework for building websites and other products such as applications and online services, divided in five planes, from bottom to top (see Figure 4.2):

FIGURE 4.2
The elements of user experience by Jesse James Garrett (Garrett, 2011).

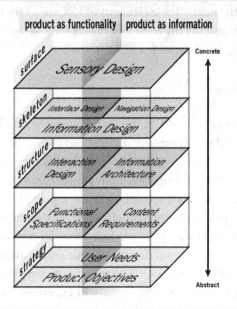

- the strategy plane, what users want to get out of the product (user needs) as well as what the business wants (business goals);
- the scope plane, defining the various features and functions of the product;
- the structure plane, defining the abstract structure of the website, service, or app. The structure plane is where interaction design and information architecture are defined;
- the skeleton plane, the concrete structure within the different screens, such as the placement of buttons, images, and blocks of text. The structure plane is where interface design (UI design) is created;
- the surface plane, defining the final look and feel. This is where visual design, sound design, and the overall aesthetics of the product happen.

Content strategy comes first. It's the most abstract plane. The product becomes more concrete and specific the higher we navigate through the planes. Each plane defines the plane right above it. Your content strategy will define the product scope, which will affect the structure your product needs to have, which in turn will constrain the skeleton, which will have an impact on the surface (what user will perceive). Garrett explains that you should not wait until you finish the work on one plane before tackling the next one. However, you should wait until a previous plane is entirely defined before *finishing* the work on the next plane (since any change of direction in a prior plane will affect the next). These elements of UX are a very useful and practical way to understand the different UX expert roles as well as how a product is built from the ground up with a UX mindset.

4.2.3 User journey

A commonly used tool in UX is the user journey, which is about defining what users want to do (i.e. problem to solve) and their expectations, how they would go about accomplishing their goal, and what they will do, think, and feel along the way (see a simplified example in Figure 4.3). User journeys are typically represented as a scenario starring a primary persona, and with a timeline that might cover different channels. For example, the user might first see an advertisement for your product on social media, go to your website to use it or buy something, download your companion app, and end up contacting your customer service via phone. It's the big picture (related to the strategy and scope planes) of what users will experience with your product ecosystem: why they would use it, how they would use it, and what they will think and feel along the way. They should be truthful and data-informed narratives that will allow the development team to visualize the journey of the user with the product ecosystem, from the user's point of view. It allows identifying pain points and areas of improvement.

4.2.4 Flow diagram (or flowchart)

A user flow diagram (or flowchart) allows clearly mapping out how a user gets to different parts of the product, and where from, thus defining the route and the means by which users can take that route. Flowcharts are less about the big picture and more about the precise information architecture (i.e. structure plane), and what will be the different screens in the interface depending on what users do. It's represented as a diagram with logic elements. For example, users arriving on the landing page of a service might have to start by logging in or, *if* they don't already have an account, *then* signing up (see a simplified example in Figure 4.4). Depending on the type of user, their goals, and the situation, their path with the product will be different. A flowchart allows ensuring all the different users, situations, and possible actions (including users' errors) are

FIGURE 4.3
Example of a user journey. (Illustration by Laura Taylor.)

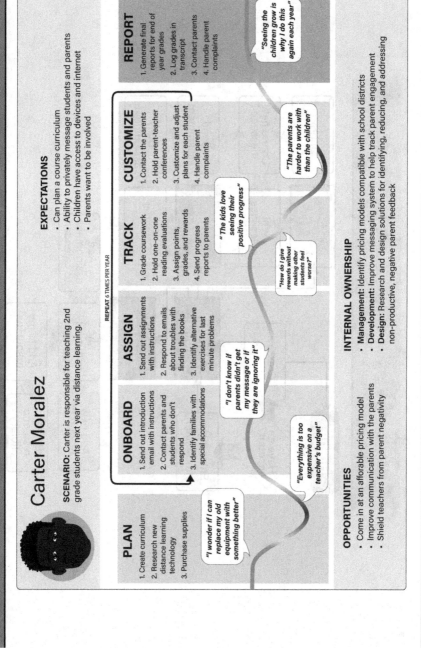

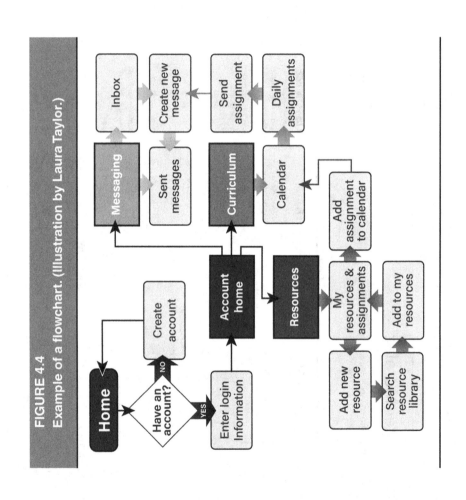

FIGURE 4.4
Example of a flowchart. (Illustration by Laura Taylor.)

accounted for. It's very useful to communicate what needs to be implemented to the entire development team, and to ensure that nothing has been overlooked.

4.2.5 Wireframe

A wireframe is the high-level visualization of the skeleton of a website or an application. Like a schematic or blueprint, it communicates the envisioned page layout, information hierarchy, user flow, and interactions. It's typically done in black and white and using very simple shapes (e.g. boxes, scribbles to represent text) to communicate what goes where and what happens when the user clicks on something. The first step can be very low-fidelity wireframes sketched by hand to explore different possible versions of the software (see Figure 4.5). Then, once a specific version is chosen, medium-fidelity wireframes can be created to communicate the vision to other team members, and validate it with stakeholders (see Figure 4.6). They can also be used to create click-through prototypes to test the interaction design with users. Sometimes higher fidelity wireframes can be created to communicate the implementation requirements more precisely to programmers.

4.2.6 Prototype

Prototypes are generally mocked-up versions of ideas for flows and layouts that are created to try them out before building the real thing. They are meant to be throw-away, allowing the team to identify issues very early, when it's cheaper and faster to correct them. Prototypes have many shapes: architects build models, painters draw sketches, sculptors create maquettes. They can have different levels of breadth (i.e. horizontal prototype) and/or depth (i.e. vertical prototype). A horizontal prototype is about experimenting with the high-level structure and scope of a product, while a vertical prototype concerns all the interactions possible with one feature. Some prototypes, called "T prototypes" (i.e. shaped like a T), can combine both breadth and depth to allow for a more precise evaluation of the system overall (Hartson and Pyla, 2012).

Prototypes can be low-fidelity (i.e. cheap and dirty), done by hand on paper or digitally using a prototyping tool when they are focused on the high-level abstract representations of a system, or high-fidelity once the product is more advanced and it makes sense to refine the design and start thinking about its aesthetics. It's usually not a good idea to make high-fidelity prototypes too soon, because it's more costly and it will be harder to make

FIGURE 4.5
Example of a sketched low-fidelity wireframe.
(Illustration by Laura Taylor.)

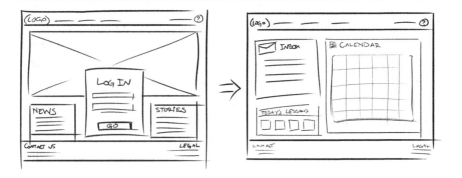

FIGURE 4.6
Example of a medium-fidelity wireframe. (Illustration by
Laura Taylor.)

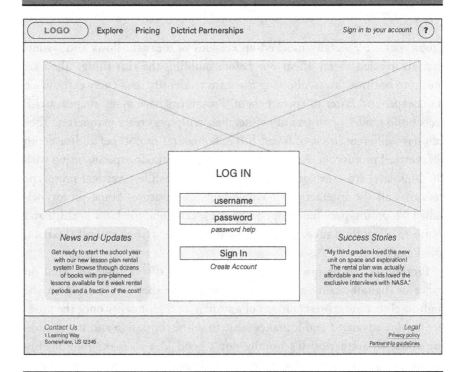

profound changes if need be, especially as you might get more attached to it if it looks too good. It can also confuse stakeholders into thinking things are further along than they *really* are and have them push for faster deadlines.

UX designers use all of the tools above (and more) to rapidly iterate and test their product vision. Testing a product in development is a critical component of the UX mindset, which leads us to user research.

4.3 UX Research (User Research)

> A user experience cannot be designed, only experienced. You are not designing or engineering or developing good usability or designing or engineering or developing a good user experience. There is no usability or user experience inside the design; they are relative to the user.
>
> *(Hartson and Pyla, 2012, p. 20)*

An experience is what happens in the user's mind as they interact with your product. UX research is about *understanding* users and *evaluating* their experience all throughout the product development stages. UX research will allow you to validate or invalidate the assumptions that you made about your users and the product itself. As UX designer Scott Jenson puts it, good UX is threatened by designers' "assertive instincts," which are strong yet biased gut feelings that can badly misguide them[1] (Jenson, 2020). The main goal of UX research is thus to keep your biases checked and your vision on track with what users truly want and need. It will also help you uncover your product's usability issues and to make the product more emotional and engaging when relevant.

While UX designers can often conduct some UX research themselves, it's recommended that they collaborate with trained researchers who will plan and execute studies. As we saw earlier, the brain has many flaws and it's very biased. It's quite easy to alter the quality of a study during its preparation, execution, analysis, or conclusion. UX researchers are trained in the scientific method; a rigorous and systematic way of acquiring knowledge about the world that greatly limits the risk of being biased by our subjective perception and mental models. For example, a leading question (e.g. "Did you find it easy to do x with the product?") can influence how users will reply and it can completely skew the results of a research. Doing science requires the utmost rigor, specifically because we are mostly unaware of

---

[1] https://jenson.org/instincts/.

our biases (i.e. *implicit* biases) and how they influence what we do or how we think.

UX researchers are also more neutral towards the product because they are not the ones building it; thus, they aren't biased with the "IKEA effect" that makes us attribute a higher value to something we participated in building (which is reflected with the expression "it's my baby" when talking about a project). Users frustrated by the design won't hurt researchers' feelings with their harsh feedback. It's not to say that user researchers aren't biased (they are humans after all), but they should be more aware of those biases and are theoretically using specific protocols that are meant to overcome human biases in data collection and analysis.

There are two main categories of research: exploratory research (i.e. generative research) to explore opportunities for innovation, and evaluative research to assess the quality of a product in development with the goal of improving it. Here are a few examples of user research methodologies.

4.3.1 Field study (or field research)

A field study is research conducted outside of the UX lab, at users' location (home, office, or any place that would make sense in the context of the product). Field studies are very important to empathize with users. There is no other way to truly understand users, their needs and desires, than making direct observations as they go about their job or other daily occupations, interviewing them, and spending time with them. Field studies are critical to the persona method, and to build the user journey map.

4.3.2 Usability testing

Usability testing is about observing real users interact with a product, the main goal being to identify and understand all friction points in order to improve its usability. It's one of the research methods the most frequently used. It implies recruiting participants who are representative of the target audience. Having a precise idea of the primary personas will then be important, as well as recruiting diverse participants from the target audience in order to uncover elements in the design that can potentially exclude certain people. The test can either be done in person, typically in a UX lab with an observation room hidden behind a one-way mirror, or done remotely (oftentimes non-moderated). In-person tests are more granular and closely moderated, and allow asking follow-up questions on the fly when an unexpected issue occurs, watching the person as they are using the product (instead of just analyzing their inputs with the product remotely), and *really* feeling people's struggle to use it as you watch from behind the one-way mirror. This is definitely a great motivator to fix usability issues. Product developers usually do not interact with participants during the test as they are too close to the product and running an experiment requires specific training to avoid biases (you don't want to accidentally influence participants' behavior and responses). The user researcher is typically the one moderating the test. As painful as it can be to watch users not understanding your product, I would recommend waiting until receiving the test report from the researcher before deciding the course of action. Again, confirmation bias (i.e. the tendency to search for and focus on data validating our preconceptions) can make you draw hasty and wrong conclusions. Watching the test is mostly useful for non-researchers to feel empathy with the people who use your product and will give you better context when you will later read the test report or receive telemetry data (see the "analytics" section below).

Participants can either be asked to use the product without any specific directions, or asked to accomplish certain tasks (i.e. task analysis). For example, when evaluating the prototype of a website meant to book concert tickets, users could be asked to search for a specific artist, find out when they are playing near them, and buy tickets. The purpose of task analyses is to analyze specific elements of the interaction design. Several versions of a prototype can be then tested to check which interaction design and information architecture work better, for example. Participants are also typically asked to give feedback and answer specific questions about the product or the prototype.

Usability tests can either be qualitative (more granular and about figuring out why users interact with the system in a certain way), or quantitative (focused on collecting metrics on a large sample of users). Qualitative usability tests are typically conducted in person and are usually done with five to eight participants. There's indeed no need for such tests to use a large sample of users, as the idea is not to gather opinions or sentiment about a product (any subjective questions do require a large sample of participants in order to get reliable results); it's about asking objective questions about the product and observing concrete behavior. For example, instead of asking vague and subjective questions such as "did you find the product efficient to accomplish your goals?" we ask participants to describe what they believe the elements of an interface mean, we ask them to show us how they think they can accomplish a task, we measure the time it takes them to do so, the number of errors along the way, and so forth. According to Nielsen (2000), five participants are enough to uncover most usability issues. Recruiting more participants for one prototype or at a specific development stage won't necessarily bring you more useful insights, while it will increase the cost and time of the test. However, keep in mind that you still need to recruit diverse participants to specifically test the accessibility and inclusiveness of your product.

During a usability test, eye-tracking and click tracking tools can be used to get a better sense of what is catching users' eyes (with the caveat that gazing at something does not necessarily mean *paying attention* to it as we saw in Chapter 3 when we explained the limitations of our working memory and attentional resources), what information and features they are thus possibly missing, and where they are clicking (which can allow you to more easily identify a non-interactive area that nonetheless looks clickable for users).

4.3.3 Rapid Iterative Testing and Evaluation (RITE)

Given that testing the same prototype with several people won't necessarily bring a lot of new insights since they mostly encounter the same usability issues, an interesting method was developed by Microsoft Games Studio researchers to increase the insights gained from each participant, called Rapid Iterative Testing and Evaluation, or RITE (Medlock et al., 2002). The idea is to test the prototype with the first participant and to immediately and quickly fix the main issues they experienced during the test before having the second participant testing the newly iterated prototype. This type of test ideally requires close collaboration between a researcher and a designer: the researcher runs the test and gives their conclusion to the designer after each participant, and the designer then quickly tweaks the prototype before the next participant arrives. Using external participants is always better, but RITEs can sometimes be conducted internally, especially in companies with a low budget. In this case, ensure that the colleagues who serve as participants are overall fitting the target audience and keep in mind that using friends, colleagues, or family introduces more biases. These people usually will put in more effort to understand the design and complete the tasks in order to please someone they know or care about, whereas an external user might have just given up.

4.3.4 Think aloud (or cognitive walkthrough)

A cognitive walkthrough is a specific way of conducting usability tests or task analyses whereby participants are asked to voice out their thought process as they are discovering an interface and interacting with a system. Think of it as narrating their experience. It's very useful to get insights into what people perceive and what they understand from the product, and how much it differs from what the product is supposed to convey.

4.3.5 Heuristic evaluation

A heuristic evaluation is usually conducted by a usability expert (or, preferentially, several) to evaluate the usability of a prototype or an early version of a product using a set of heuristics (such as the Nielsen's usability heuristics we saw earlier). This is the only methodology that does not require actual users to run. It can be useful when the product is in a very rough state (which can make it difficult to test with users), or when you cannot conduct UX tests. While usability experts (who are often user researchers) can uncover some of the more common usability issues and clear the ground, their heuristic evaluation can only hypothesize what a user's actual behavior will be and therefore can never replace UX tests.

4.3.6 Survey

Surveys are used to collect data on users or potential users, either for exploratory questions or product evaluation. They can be very insightful but they come with caveats. First of all, you need to avoid leading questions, and second of all, humans are not good at understanding why they feel a certain way about something. If you ask people what they feel about the product, don't take their answer at face value; it will be your job to figure out *why* they feel this way (and you typically will need other research methodologies to find out). Do not ask users for advice or about the future, such as "would you buy this product?," because humans are also not good at projecting what they will do, as you surely know if you ever made resolutions at the beginning of a new year and didn't *really* follow through.

4.3.7 Focus group

A focus group is when you invite several potential users from your target audience to discuss how they feel about a competitive product, what frustration they encounter when trying to accomplish a task that your product is supposed to make easier, what they would expect from such a product, and so forth. It's an exploratory tool. Again, the idea here is not to ask users what you should design, but to uncover their problems, their needs, their desires, and their expectations so that *you* can figure out how you can make their lives easier and have a better understanding of their mental models. Focus groups are very hard to run properly, as interacting directly with a group of people introduces more biases than having them individually answer a standardized survey. Interviews, focus groups, and any research methodology that implies discussing with people must be conducted by highly trained researchers.

4.3.8 Analytics

Analytics is about collecting data remotely from people using the product *and* making sense of it. This type of data is called telemetry data and it's currently very *en vogue*, although many companies tend to collect way more data than what is justified for their needs, and tend to forget that the important part relies in the *analysis*, which should be conducted by a data scientist or analyst. Indeed, companies tend to be "data-driven," which means that they merely react to data collected without first *really* trying to figure out what it means. Data by itself is not information, and information is only useful if it provides the insights you need to solve specific problems. Telemetry data is very efficient at telling you *what* users are doing on a large scale, but not necessarily *why*, as it lacks context (which can be gained with in-person UX tests). Furthermore, manipulating data is very delicate (e.g. deciding what data to collect and how, verifying and cleaning the data, running the adequate model to analyze it), and you should not do it unless you're properly trained in data science, otherwise you might end up finding a pattern in the data that doesn't actually exist, or is not significant or meaningful. You could very well fool yourself, or get fooled by someone else using dubious data presented as "scientific evidence" to convince you of something (see Bergstrom and West, 2020, to learn how to identify bullshit despite the veneer of numbers and statistics).

Analytics are currently mostly used by the "business intelligence" team, who is focused on supporting business decision making. Typical metrics collected are "daily active users" (how many different people are using the product every day), "retention rate" (proportion of users coming back the next day, within a week, or within a month), and the "conversion rate" (how many users are buying something on the platform). Those metrics, called key performance indicators (KPIs), don't necessarily matter too much for UX professionals as they don't reveal what experience users are having and if this experience is satisfying over the long term. For example, users might be coming back every day not because the product or service is useful to them but because they can't figure out how to accomplish a task. If you have ever hung up on an automated phone system and called back to start over again because the menu options are confusing, then you have likely experienced this. If the company measures success by how many calls aren't routed to live customer service agents, they may come to the false conclusion that their automated system is helping their users. The reality is that the issues "resolved" by the automated system are actually multiple calls from the same frustrated users hanging up and calling again. Or users might "convert" not because they *really* wanted to buy something or subscribe to something but because they clicked on the wrong button (or because a dark pattern was used, see Chapter 5 on ethics). Also, looking at those metrics in isolation can make you miss important insights. For example, maybe the conversion rate has been increasing lately, but your requests for refunds have also increased at a similar rate.

Looking at numbers going up or down is not very useful if you don't have hypotheses and you're collecting precise data in order to answer your research questions. Besides, UX professionals typically need more granular data than business intelligence. We might want to know what features were used and not used, where did users click, or how much time they spent on a screen on average. UX researchers can often partner with data analysts to combine quantitative data with qualitative data and gain a better understanding of the main issues users can encounter and why.

UX research is a powerful tool but the data collected can easily be biased… and bad data is actually worse than no data because it can lead you to false conclusions. I would urge you to entrust academically trained researchers (oftentimes coming from human factors research or experimental psychology) and experienced data scientists with your research needs. Empower these people and collaborate with them to explore the relevant questions and get the answers you need to provide you with actionable insights. Researchers, analysts, and product creators should work together to define hypotheses and to prepare the research in a way that will fit your milestones and timeline. If you are a product creator, you have the curse of knowledge (i.e. you know your product too well). Furthermore, confirmation bias is looming over each and every one of us. Mix research methodologies and combine different data points (including from customer service) in order to gain a more accurate perspective on how users experience your product. Science is powerful, but it's a delicate and rigorous enterprise, and it's important to understand and respect how it works.

4.4 UX Strategy and Maturity

Having a UX mindset isn't solely about understanding the science, processes, and methodologies used by UX professionals, it's also about developing a strategy. UX strategy goes beyond product strategy (i.e. whom it is for, what problems it solves, what experience it should offer, how to build and market it). It's about having a vision for the entire user journey with the product ecosystem, and even with the company as a whole. Apple is often mentioned as a company that has had a strong UX strategy for a long time. It's reflected in their slogan (i.e. "think different"), in their stores, in the way products are boxed, in the design of the products themselves, and in their customer service. Of course this is not to say that everything Apple creates has a perfect UX, far from it, but it means that they have a strong vision of what experience they want to offer to their customers and users at every step of the journey.

To develop a strong UX strategy, it's also important to focus on the company structure and processes. Is the company diverse and inclusive? Does it have strong values well communicated and enforced (such as striving for inclusion and accessibility)? Does it promote design thinking and experimentation? Does it embrace failure as part of the learning and design processes? Do employees feel valued and autonomous? Can everyone bring insights into the table or are executives making all the decisions in a silo? Is science valued? Are UX experts well represented and assimilated across the company? Do they actually have a background in human factors psychology, human-computer interaction, research, or HCD, or is the term UX in their title just for show? Are UX processes well implemented in the company and given sufficient resources (for example, are UX tests fully integrated in the production cycle)? Is there team alignment regarding who the users are and what core experience is intended for them, and are there strategies in place to ensure this alignment is maintained? Are discoveries and insights shared across teams so that more profound changes can be made that would positively impact the experience of users across products (such as an architecture shared by several products)? Is the UX of the tools used by the company also considered and addressed? These are examples of the questions you need to ask yourself to establish a UX strategy on your product team, and in your company. Let's take the example of such a strategy, focused on defining the best way to foster a UX mindset in production.

4.4.1 Lean UX

One of the key elements of a UX strategy is to have an efficient approach to production management. Today, the approach called "Lean UX" is a popular one in Agile development teams. Contrary to the "waterfall" model of product management that has rigid linear stages of development with a gate blocking the transition to the next stage, Agile development is more dynamic and flexible. It focuses on collaboration across teams and on an incremental approach. The idea of an incremental approach is that if you want to build a new online shopping platform offering a lot of different products (say, Amazon), you start small to demonstrate the value of the vision and put the management of the whole user journey to test (i.e. you first build a platform to sell books online). The work in an Agile product cycle is broken down in smaller chunks tackled in "sprints" that run for a few weeks. With a care for UX and given the right accommodations (especially regarding sprint durations that can be too short to allow for enough time for experimentation) UX processes can blossom. More specifically, Agile managers need to understand the "lean" approach to fully benefit from a UX mindset.

The lean approach (or lean thinking) is inspired from Japanese management methods. More specifically, it's inspired from lean manufacturing at Toyota (spearheaded by industrial engineers Shigeo Shingo and Taiichi Ohno) that allegedly saved the company from bankruptcy and turned it into one of the top leading automotive manufacturers in the world. In a nutshell, lean thinking favors fast iteration and customer insights, which resonates well with design thinking. This approach is particularly important for startups and companies who want to innovate. Inventing a new technology or proposing a new service or application is not enough to be innovative. Innovation emerges when a new technology is desirable *and* meets people's needs and wants. Thus, it's better to get a simpler and smaller version of the envisioned product out of the door early to test your hypotheses about your product or service in a very concrete way, with real people.

The entrepreneur Eric Ries has championed the concept of lean startups. In his book, *The Lean Startup* (2011), Ries talks about the importance of building a *minimum viable product* (MVP), the smallest version of a functional product that takes the least amount of effort to put together, yet can yield very insightful feedback from actual users. The MVP is the fastest and cheapest version of the product you want to build, with only the most essential features to begin with, so that you can test it with your customers and learn. It allows you to start small (thus limiting the time and money investment to a minimum), quickly assess if the product finds its audience and answers people's problems and, if so, how to fine-tune its way to commercial success and make it grow carefully. If not, you'll be able to recognize sooner when you need to pivot and limit the damage to your company. "Lean thinking defines value as providing benefit to the customer; anything else is waste" (Ries, 2011, p. 46). This notion of waste is very important in lean thinking; the idea is to identify where your company is producing waste (work that isn't valuable to your customers) and to get rid of it.

Lean UX is thus about fostering a UX mindset within a lean approach to product development management. Given that production costs can be very high (even for digital products), the idea is to first build a MVP as fast as possible, get it out of the door, and see how people use it. Simply put, it's a design thinking process where the product is launched while still very small so that it can be refined with user feedback in a real-life situation. It's a way to test your hypotheses.

The video game industry, although not always very lean or very versed in the UX mindset, has increasingly been releasing games in "Beta" stage (meaning that the game is functional but not fine-tuned or ready to be launched), during which a few thousands of interested players can play it for free, therefore providing useful telemetry data that can be analyzed (hopefully with insights from in-person UX tests, often called "playtests" in the game industry), and feedback through online surveys. The massively successful game *Fortnite* (Epic Games), on which I worked from 2013 to 2017 as director of UX, was notoriously developed and refined using this approach. The game was opened to a limited number of players very early on (when all features were not even built yet) for a few consecutive weeks in a row in regular "online tests" for over 2 years. The first online test happened in December 2014, and *Fortnite* was released in early access for everyone in July 2017. These regular tests allowed us to not only fine-tune the gameplay but also check the publishing pipeline, the game servers, the management of the player community, and so forth. It was through this iterative approach that *Fortnite* could be developed with a strong UX mindset and strategy.

Lean UX for online products means having a service approach (hence the term "Games as a service" or "GaaS" in the video game industry), with constant

updates allowing refining the product with its users. It's about acknowledging with humility that no matter how great you think your product idea is,
you are probably making many wrong assumptions and you need to focus on
how users experience the product, and on what *they* feel about it. In her book
UX for Lean Startups (2018), engineer and designer Laura Klein explains:

> Instead of thinking of a product as a series of features to be built, Lean
> UX looks at a product as a set of hypotheses to be validated. In other
> words, we don't assume that we know what the user wants. We do cus-
> tomer interviews and research in order to develop a hypothesis about
> what a customer might want, and then we test this hypothesis in various
> ways to see if we were right. And we keep going every time we make a
> change in the product.

Don't start with product features. Start with hypotheses, and ask yourself
why your product would be meaningful in people's lives. This will allow you
to understand what problems your users have, and generate ideas to possibly
fix them with your product. Then, you will more easily define the metrics
(from UX test data to telemetry data) that will validate or invalidate your
assumptions, and that will guide you all throughout the development process
and beyond. This, in essence, is what UX strategy is about.

Lean UX and having a UX strategy overall will provide you with a key
competitive edge. In order to foster such a deep UX mindset in your company, you need to advance its UX maturity.

4.4.2 UX maturity stages

To offer a framework for UX maturity development in a company, Jakob
Nielsen proposed a UX maturity framework on the website nngroup.com
(Nielsen, 2006a, 2006b), which was very recently updated and consolidated
into a six-stage model (Pernice et al., 2021):

- **Stage 1: Absent**. UX is rejected or ignored, and UX misconceptions are widespread. In companies at this level, you can hear people saying things like "we don't have any issues with our products
  and customers are happy, we don't need this." The main barrier is a
  lack of education about UX, which can be addressed by advocating
  for UX, explaining what it is and is not (Chapters 1 and 2), and
  explaining the limitations of the brain (Chapter 3).
- **Stage 2: Limited**. UX work is rare or lacks importance. Companies
  typically have awareness of UX at this stage, and say that it's important to their business, but don't *really* plan for UX practices in the

schedule and budget. You might hear things like "users come first," but what this means specifically is not concretely established. This stage is the lip-service level of UX. The main barrier is a lack of know-how and can be overcome by applying UX methodologies on small elements to establish quick wins (such as running a simple usability test and use low-hanging fruit to improve the design of a product; Chapter 4).

- **Stage 3: Emergent**. UX work is present but happens inconsistently. The efforts are oftentimes carried out by a few UX advocates and don't have the full support at an organizational level. You might hear things like "UX research is great and we would do it if we had the time, but we need to do without it given our tight deadline." The main obstacle is thinking that UX is just one step in the development process instead of thinking that UX *is* the process. It can be strenuous to overcome this stage, and it requires promoting UX as a mindset and a strategy. Quantification of UX methodologies to measure results and progress can help moving forward, as well as trying to get more UX professionals hired across the company.

- **Stage 4: Structured**. UX work is used semi-systematically and the organization recognizes the value of UX. UX teams are established, and UX processes are used all throughout the product development stages. However, UX strategy is not full-blown and resources can be allocated inefficiently. Some teams (such as executive or marketing team) might not be fully comfortable with UX and while they support UX processes for product development, they tend ignore them for business and marketing decisions. UX is valued, but does not have the same weight as business intelligence or finance teams. The main tool for advancement is to link UX processes to KPIs to show the return on investment of the UX mindset at all levels.

- **Stage 5: Integrated**. UX work is effective and pervasive. KPIs are linked to UX practices, and UX strategy has the same weight as the business strategy. However, this is when UX practices can be seen as a business asset only, thus losing sight of users' best interests which is actually what's core to UX. The company is business-driven and uses UX to mostly serve business goals and drive profitability.

- **Stage 6: User-driven**. UX is the norm and a culture. There's dedication to UX at all levels. The business vision is user-centered design (Chapter 5).

I would argue that to be considered at Stage 6, the company also needs to be fully considering ethics, inclusion, and accessibility for their products, their ecosystem, and in their workplace. A list of company values should be established and enforced, and ethical lines that the company will not cross defined. For example: "Even if the company falls under profitability, dark patterns should never be used" (see the next chapter about ethics). There should be a clear win-win balance between users, business goals, and even employees' health. Humans come first; users' best interests are truly prioritized, with the goal of developing a long-lasting and respectful relationship with customers.

It takes many years to climb up these stages and progression at the higher ones is particularly slow. To move your company forward, focus on fighting misconceptions, establishing techniques, developing processes, and linking the latter to KPIs. Hopefully, you will reach executive levels when company heads truly understand the benefit of having a UX strategy, and don't shy away from ethics and inclusion.

5

Ethics and the UX Mindset

UX is becoming trendy; many job descriptions have the term "UX" in their titles, and an increasing number of businesses now understand the value of UX practices. Except that they don't, in many cases. There's a very concerning trend of considering UX practices, and the cognitive science behind it as an efficient tool to "get" and "hook" people, "captivate" their attention, or make them "addicted" (we'll see later that this term is misused) to a service, and overall just seduce people to consume goods and retain them on a platform with mind tricks. The cold cynicism of the vernacular used in business and marketing today can be chilling. But the worst part is that this vocabulary is starting to be linked to UX practitioners, affecting the very people in a company who are primarily caring for users' best interests. IDEO's chair Tim Brown noticed that "(...) design is being used to seduce us to the addictions [sic] of social media, artificially intelligent services, mobile games, and other technological enticements laid before us" (Brown, 2019, p. 4). This sad outcome can sometimes be the result of poor design, and thus be a UX failure. When we create a product or service, we must ensure that it will efficiently solve users' needs *and* also be safe and inclusive. Anticipating issues that would compromise users' best interests is *entirely* part of our responsibilities as UX practitioners (and I would argue company executives and business sharehold-ers as well). It's bad enough to have a negative impact on people's lives unin-tentionally, but this outcome can actually be deliberate and thus completely betrays the UX mindset. To use Brown's words again, "(...) human-centered design can be applied as an antidote to the cold dominance of technology and its inherent bias to replace or devalue the contributions of people" (p. 4). UX is fundamentally humanistic, and the fact that many people—and even some so-called UX professionals themselves—conveniently forget this core tenet is

DOI: 10.1201/9781003215370-6

profoundly disconcerting. If you have "UX" or a related-term in your job title, you must be the user's advocate. Maybe the term "user" in UX which replaced "human" in *human* factors and *human*-centered design is contributing to losing sight of what UX is about. Or maybe it's a victim of its own success. These past years, its popularity grew much faster than its understanding. Recruiters are told to find UX profiles, while UX maturity overall is still very low, which means that UX misconceptions are still widely spread and it can be confused with either UI design at low maturity stages, or with business intelligence (i.e. mainly concerned with maximizing profitability) at higher stages. As a result, recruiters and hiring managers don't necessarily know what sort of profiles to look for and since finding UX professionals is extremely difficult today, some job seekers are just tempted to add "UX" in their resume without having the relevant expertise or background, or after taking a UX class of just a few hours or days. Anyone can transition into a UX position of course but not without adequate training or expertise (which typically take years to acquire because humans are complex). The bottom line is that we are currently in a situation where UX is highly desirable while not understood, even by some newly appointed "UX" professionals (not to mention untrained professionals who just add UX-related skills on their resume to be more attractive). To make things worse, ill-intended people are using the label UX to sell their services while only focusing on improving business metrics and ignoring the key component of a UX mindset: minding the user's best interests. Claiming to be a UX professional while making business decisions at the expense of users' best interests, either intentionally or unintentionally, is unethical and can be both damaging to UX advocates and the industry they work in.

There's a growing uncomfortable feeling expressed by some UX, HCD, or human factors trailblazers that something has gone wrong. UX designer Jesse James Garrett very recently expressed his discomfort in a moving piece[1] for *Fast Company* (2021). For Garrett, the values of the UX mindset were promising, as it entailed

> a degree of respect, compassion, and simple humility toward the people who use what we make, and the ways in which their lives and experiences may shape their behavior to look very different from our own. More exposure to this kind of thinking, the theory went, would lead to more demand for it, and the rising tide of human-centered design would pave the way for human-centered enterprises.

---

[1] https://www.fastcompany.com/90642462/i-helped-pioneer-ux-design-what-i-see-today-horrifies-me.

What we got instead are tech companies (but not only) mostly obsessed about *disrupting* everything (even what previously worked) and focused on retention and conversion rates. Tools traditionally used by UX professionals were taken advantage of to accomplish these business goals without even pausing a minute to ensure that the developed products would truly improve people's lives. Not to mention the long-term impact on the environment. Increasingly, the label UX is now wrongly attached to these practices. We are currently witnessing a corruption of UX values and principles in service of profits. In many ways, UX has become this juicy cherry that businesses happily chew to suck out all its sweet sugar and business-healthy fibers, only to spit out the stone holding its humanistic values. If you are reading these lines, it is imperative that you understand the importance of embracing the ethics of UX as the central component of the UX mindset. Trends move fast, and new technologies are constantly put on the market. Genuinely caring about building a long-term respectful relationship with your fellow humans (also known as customers and users) and their fragile environment will stand out among the competition.

Beyond the deontological issues of watering down the UX mindset, there are additional ethical concerns that tech and design overall bring into our society, which we will now address.

5.1 Influence in Design: Good UX, Bad UX, Nudges, and Dark Patterns

One of the most important things to consider in UX is that a design can never be neutral; it will always influence its users one way or another. Even seeing a simple handle on a door will influence you to grab it and pull. Influencing people's behaviors or emotions (in the case of art and entertainment) is not an ethical concern by itself. It all depends on the intention behind the design and the impact on users. I classify the influence of design on people's lives into four main categories:

- **Good UX:** this is when a design works as intended, is intuitive, and improves people's lives in various degrees. At the lowest degree, people can accomplish their goals easily without encountering any friction points (opening a door, executing a task, or understanding a piece of information) and at the highest level, a design might greatly improve their lives (e.g. automating a strenuous task). Good UX is intentional, and it entails having empathy, respect, and compassion for users.

- **Bad UX** (or #UXfail): this occurs when users encounter frustrations with a product or service. They cannot easily accomplish their tasks, are confused, or cannot even use a service because of accessibility issues. Bad UX is usually not intentional. It could be the result of compromises that had to be made because of production or engineering constraints, or it could be the result of bad decision-making, or neglect of the human-centered design process (or absence of such process). UX professionals strive to identify, understand, and fix UX issues to avoid bad UX as much as possible (given the business constraints). Bad UX can sometimes be borderline intentional, when UX matters less than short-term profits and malpractice follows (e.g. when a building is built with cheap material and without following security rules to cut down on cost).

- **Nudges**: this term can be used to express different types of intentional behavioral influence and is sometimes called "choice architecture" (see Thaler and Sunstein, 2008), but I will use it here exclusively to indicate a design that is consciously made to change people's behaviors with a benevolent intention: either for the long-term benefit of the user and/ or the greater good. Road safety and gamification belong in this category. For example, a speed bump is *nudging* drivers to slow down for the security of all, and a video game in augmented reality with zombies chasing players nudges them to run and exercise. While nudges can be considered as being good UX at its peak (e.g. health applications helping people taking their medicine or exercising), it sometimes implies a not-so-good experience for the user on the short-term as long-term benefits (or greater good) are favored. For example, it's not necessarily a good experience to drive over speed bumps, or to hear an annoying beep if we don't fasten our seatbelt, but the overall goal is benevolent. It can also be less convenient to use a glass container instead of a plastic one, or to have a purchase delivered in a few days instead of a few hours, but it's more beneficial for the environment and thus for all of humanity in the long term. Of course, human factor researchers and practitioners have traditionally been concerned about designing safe systems and protocols that increase cognitive or physical load to avoid dangerous human errors. Yet it is useful to consider a specific category for products and systems that aim to change the behavior of a population, especially when it's for the greater good whether it is to convince people to get vaccinated, wear masks, exercise regularly, stop smoking, eat less meat, and so forth. This category (and the next) requires a more intense ethical scrutiny: in a democracy, nudges require enlightened consent and the approval of the majority, which can sometimes (surprise!) be neglected. In fact, the main criticism of the nudge approach is its potential for paternalism.

- **Dark patterns**: this term, coined by UX designer Harry Brignull, describes a design that is purposely deceitful with the conscious intent of maximizing a company's profits at the expense of users. These are the ones "tricking" people to profit off of them. Dark patterns are intentionally malevolent (with various severity of consequences) and thus constitute an anti-UX mindset in essence. Let's take a closer look at them.

5.2 Dark Patterns: A Malevolent and Anti-UX Influence

People and companies behind dark patterns do not care about users' best interests. Or at least they care about their business' interests much more. A dark pattern is a design purposely tricking people to buy something they didn't *really* want or need, subscribe to something without them realizing, or give away their data that is then sold to third parties or used for advertising without full consent. Take what we could consider as a a dark pattern that was used by Amazon.com in the past. When users were done shopping on the website, they clicked on the cart icon to check out. A screen would then appear with a bunch of text and a big orange button (i.e. "call to action") labeled "GET STARTED" (see Hodent, 2019, for a capture of this screen[2]). As you now know, we have very scarce attentional resources, thus aren't carefully paying attention to every single element of a screen, less of all a block of text, especially when we're focused on a task such as checking out and moving on with our day. The problem is that if users clicked on the big orange button, they would not only check out but also sign up to the Amazon Prime service (which is a paid monthly subscription). Carefully

---

[2]https://celiahodent.com/ethics-in-the-videogame-industry/.

reading the text before clicking might have helped users realize what was about to happen, but of course this isn't what most of us do. This is breaking the first Nielsen's usability heuristic "visibility of system status;" it's not entirely clear and transparent for users what will happen if they click on the big orange button (or it necessitates too much cognitive load to understand it). Users who did realize what was going on and wanted to check out *without* signing up to Amazon Prime had to click on a much smaller hyperlink on the left (harder to aim at and click on as we can anticipate using Fitts's law). On top of it, the hyperlink text said "No thanks, I do not want to save $18.95," thus potentially guilt-tripping users by insinuating that they are a bit stupid to miss out on the discount offered with the Amazon Prime membership (while not mentioning at that time how much the membership itself costs after the free trial ends). And nowhere on this screen could you find a button clearly labeled "Check Out," which would have much more likely fit what users want to do at this stage.

A dark pattern uses *some* of the same knowledge and techniques as human-centered design. The most important difference is the *intention* behind the design: it's clearly not caring for users' best interests (e.g. while many users might have subscribed to the paid membership without realizing it, it could take relatively more effort to cancel the subscription once they realized what happened and were not ok with it). Dark patterns are subtle scams that often violate usability guidelines, more specifically the importance of making a system transparent for users. Deception is opaque. Another classic example is when you buy a plane ticket and at the moment you need to pay, an automatically checked option makes you add insurance for your trip. If you don't carefully read the fine prints or check the price again before paying, you might end up paying more for an insurance you didn't *really* want to buy. You will find the different types of dark patterns and examples on Harry Brignull's website DarkPatterns.org.

Some people call dark patterns "dark UX," but this doesn't make much sense when we know that UX is a mindset with the intention of improving people's lives. Thus, "dark UX" is an oxymoron. It would be like calling someone who used a drug to intentionally poison someone else a "dark pharmacist." Or calling a pickpocketer a "dark magician." Of course, the issue is that most people don't *really* understand what UX values are, which is why UX is starting to be associated with malevolent practices that are the exact opposite of what it is all about.

There's also a tendency to call dark patterns "manipulative designs." The problem with this term is that, technically, all designs are manipulative. A mentalist manipulates your attention and memory, a painter manipulates your perception, a filmmaker uses close ups and sad music to manipulate your emotion, a teacher manipulates students' minds with education. Designers, like most humans, also manipulate other people's minds in their job. Even seeing a handle on a door manipulates you to grab and pull. You might want to point out that we usually employ the term "manipulation" when we mean a *malevolent* influence or persuasion, except that this is actually not always the case. For instance, we casually say that magicians "manipulate" us to do their "mind tricks." Is this a problem? Not if you consent to the magic show and they don't take advantage of this manipulation to steal your watch in the process. Persuasion, influence, manipulation... all these words sound scary and are used to create and feed moral panics around technology, which, ironically, is also a type of malevolent manipulation (e.g. "clickbait"). It's not the manipulation itself that is necessarily problematic. It's the *intention* behind the manipulation.

Pointing fingers at UX professionals because they use the same knowledge, tools, or processes as dark-pattern troublemakers is not only absurd, it's counterproductive. UX practitioners are actually the only business professionals who have users' best interests as part of their job description, theoretically. This is why it's so important for UX professionals and advocates to remind (or teach) everyone of our core purpose, and to defend UX values.

5.3 Shady Practices and the Rise of the "attention economy"

While dark patterns can be fairly straightforward to identify and are clearly anti-UX, many other practices aren't exactly deceiving, yet are still questionable and should be debated among UX practitioners. These are what I would call "gray area patterns," or shady practices, flirting with blurry ethical lines. Take grocery stores. Placing the most commonly desired products at the rear of the store in the hope of luring customers into buying things they didn't initially intend to buy is an example of a gray area practice. It's not fully a dark pattern because the deception is not blatant, yet it is clearly about increasing the physical load (thus violating a usability guideline) in an attempt to maximize profits at the expense of users. As you can see in this example, gray area patterns and questionable practices weren't created by the tech industry. It's a long tradition that has been infecting most industries. Some might even call them "good business practices" or "smart marketing tactics."

Here are just a few other examples of shady practices exploiting our mind flaws and biases at the expense of users with the intention of increasing profits:

- **Guilt tripping**: When users don't do a certain behavior (e.g. haven't used a service for a long time), a sad message or image is used to provoke a feeling of guilt, in the hope of influencing the user to engage with the product and service again. For example, the image of a cute character crying if we haven't used a language learning app for a long time, or a sad message displayed when we attempt to unsubscribe to a service.
- **Capitalizing on loss aversion**: Users are told that if they don't do a certain action or buy a certain thing, they will lose a benefit. For example, losing your frequent flyer status if you don't buy a plane ticket before the year is over, or even losing your cumulated points in a completely artificial system (such as Snapchat's "Snapstreaks") if you don't chat with your social media friends every day.
- **Capitalizing on the fear of missing out (FOMO)**: Users are told that they have an amazing opportunity to get juicy discounts, which they will miss out if they don't act fast. All sales discounts operate on FOMO. FOMO typically works well with scarcity (i.e. "Hurry! There's only one left in stock"), and when scarcity is entirely fabricated (i.e. the stock level of the item is actually high), it becomes a dark pattern.
- **Capitalizing on the status quo bias (or default bias)**: We mostly prefer to keep things the way they are and, given the choice between doing something and not doing anything, we will usually opt for inaction. This bias is why most people keep the default settings on their devices (and thus why default settings should be carefully thought through). Using an "opt-out" option is an example exploiting the default bias: having to check a box to *not* receive a newsletter is an opt-out option (the opt-in version would be to check the box *if* we want to receive the newsletter). Auto-play is another potentially shady practice to keep us engaged with a platform, such as Netflix or YouTube (or a multiplayer video game): it forces us to act to stop something like playing a video, which we are less likely to do because of the status quo bias. One last version of this is to offer a 1-month free subscription. Of course, you are told that if you don't like the service you can opt-out at any point. Except that, we will have a tendency to just keep rolling with the service (and in a month, we might even forget that we subscribed to this service since our memory is fallible).

Some of these practices can be good UX if the intent is to avoid a potentially costly error for the user. Other times, it can be justified in terms of business constraints, such as a clearance sale when a physical store needs to clear out their inventory. But in many cases, these practices are more questionable. And some of them are at play in what is often called today the "attention economy." As we saw in Chapter 3, our attentional resources are scarce while there are many apps, services, and products that require our attention to sell and be used. Thus, many companies are competing to grab and keep our attention, so that we hopefully won't check out a competitor. Features such as bottomless scrolling (such as on Facebook or Twitter), auto-play, or push notifications (used by all social media and many mobile apps) can influence us to engage or stay engaged with a platform even if we didn't have a clear intention to do so initially. Again, competing for attention is nothing new and certainly wasn't invented by tech companies. Advertisement is entirely about grabbing people's attention unwillingly while commuting, listening to music, watching TV, or browsing social media. What is new though is that we now have a device that is always with us and can grab our attention at all times: our smartphones. While it can be a good UX to receive an *opt-in* push notification on our phone to remember to drink water, exercise, or take our medication, it becomes problematic to be constantly distracted without our full consent. Attentional resources are scarce, and we must define when good UX stops and when a shady practice starts.

It can be surprisingly difficult to identify where the ethical lines should be drawn. Take a punch card: every time you buy a sandwich at your local takeout restaurant, you receive a stamp. After 25 stamps, you are offered a free drink and desert. Like all loyalty programs, this capitalizes on the "goal-gradient" effect (proposed by psychologist Clark L. Hull) stating that the closer we get to a goal the more motivated we are to pursue the goal. Since it's technically capitalizing on a human bias, should we consider this a shady practice? On the other hand, it's nice to feel valued as a regular customer and we might even expect such rewards, and thus feel neglected when we don't receive them. So punch cards might be a good win-win example (it's good both for the user and the business). Imagine now that the punch card is only valid for 1 month. After this time, you need to get a brand new card and start accumulating stamps from the very beginning. This starts to feel like a shady practice now, doesn't it? It capitalizes on loss aversion, and instead of rewarding engagement it is in effect *punishing disengagement* (i.e. if you don't eat nearly every day at this place, you won't get your reward). This is the main problem with social media and video games today: their design can sometimes use shady practices to punish disengagement. While it's a great thing to be able to connect with our friends even if we're physically distant, fearing to miss out on amazing events with exclusive rewards that will only happen in the current "season" might be crossing the line. The devil is in the detail, which is why it can actually be very difficult to define good ethical standards in tech and entertainment, and why we need a nuanced discussion on this topic instead of wrapping it all up in a moral panic basket.

There are more ethical concerns to consider with tech and other products, but my point here is to give you a primer so that you can start thinking about your events, offers, discounts, and other features with an ethical lens. It's not because your competitors are doing it that you should mindlessly copy them. If you care about UX, you must also care about ethics and consider the subtle psychological pressures exploiting human biases meant to improve business metrics. UX is not about exploiting humans; it's about improving their lives. So ask yourself if the potentially shady feature you want to add will *really* be meaningful to users—in which case it can be a win-win situation—or if it's just an attention grabber to improve your metrics.

5.4 Of "addiction" and "dopamine shots"

I mentioned earlier that the use of the term "addiction" to talk about shady practices in tech, social media, or games is problematic. Indeed, an addiction is a pathology that has a precise clinical definition (albeit debated among scholars), and being highly engaged with a platform or device is not enough to make someone an addict. An addiction generally refers to a condition characterized by the compulsive use of a substance, such as nicotine or opioids, despite harmful consequences. The substance can create a physical dependence, such as heroin binding to opioid receptors in the brain, thus creating a surge of pleasurable sensation. Other substances don't disturb the balance of hormonal and neuronal systems as dramatically but can create a dependence that is mainly psychological. The substance by itself is not enough to create an addiction, which is more typically the result of an encounter between a substance, a person (e.g. personality traits), and a context (e.g. stressful environment, neglect, grief). Other addictions that are not substance-related are said to be "behavioral," such as gambling. In fact, "gambling disorder" is the only behavioral addiction confirmed in the DSM-5 *(Diagnostic and Statistical Manual of Mental Disorders)*, the manual used to diagnose mental disorders. In 2017, the World Health Organization announced that they would identify "gaming disorder" as a new disorder, but it resulted in some controversy among scholars who pointed out that this new nomenclature was premature given the current state of research on pathological gaming. At the time of writing, "tech addiction," "screen addiction," or "social media" addiction aren't currently clinically recognized as specific addictions needing specific treatment. Which is not to say that some people do not suffer from a problematic relationship with these products, but casually comparing problematic use of technology to substance addiction is stigmatizing the billions of gamers and smartphone users while downplaying true addiction suffering. Besides, like with substance addiction, a technology or a platform is not creating an addiction by itself. Addiction is a *process* happening between three actors: the object, the person, and the context. In its clinical meaning, addiction isn't something that can be designed, nor should it be a desired goal despite what some games and apps boasting about their "addictive features" might say.

Furthermore, the whole pseudoscientific narrative around "dopamine shots" distributed by tech is not constructive. Simply put, the dopamine system in the midbrain is thought to be a reward prediction system influencing our motivation to doing certain activities that could lead to a reward. Addictive drugs are known to provoke an imbalance to this dopaminergic system. While it's true that playing video games has been shown to increase the levels of dopamine in the brain by about 100%, for example (Koepp et al., 1998), "natural" rewards such as food or sex also increase dopamine levels by 150%–300% (Allerton and Blake, 2008), and meditation was found to increase dopamine levels by 65% (Kjaer et al., 2002). As a comparison, methamphetamines increase dopamine levels by over 1,000%. Neuroscience is very trendy and some influential tech leaders have a tendency to throw neurobullshit here and there to sound fancier in their TED talks, or in an attempt to put more weight on an ethical issue that shouldn't need neurobollocks to be deemed important. The truth is less dramatic: we still don't clearly understand the role of certain neurochemicals in addiction, such as dopamine or serotonin. In fact, the level of dopamine elicited by a drug (e.g. cocaine or alcohol) does *not* predict how many people will get addicted to the drug, or the severity of the addiction (Foddy, 2016). Reducing problematic use of technology to "dopamine shots" is therefore a gross oversimplification that doesn't help anyone; meanwhile, it's feeding the growing moral panic around tech. Insubstantial documentaries are scaring people by pretending that technology is "hacking" our brain in a physiological sense to completely take control of people, framing this as a "dilemma" for the tech industry.

This is nonsense. Worse, it's ironically a shady pattern using sensationalism and fear to grab people's attention. Yes, understanding better the conditions that could potentially lead to a pathological use of tech or video games is warranted, and there absolutely are ethical issues that need to be discussed, but fear-mongering is actually one of them. No one is using dopamine shots to create addiction with a product. We have enough UX problems to solve in tech (such as discrimination perpetuated by artificial intelligence); there's no need to create a panic based on fake science on top of it.

5.5 Inclusion and Accessibility

I mentioned several times in this book that UX professionals care about improving the life of *all* people, not just a subcategory of users who fit within your preconception of who will be using your product (i.e. likely someone who looks like you because of the egocentric bias). The problem is that any design has the potential to exclude some people. A design conveying information via colors only will exclude colorblind people. A video game that conveys emotion via music or sound design only will exclude people who are deaf or hard of hearing. It's entirely part of our job to identify the barriers of access and enjoyment that a design creates to tear down all unnecessary barriers. For example, a staircase creates a barrier that can be removed by adding a proper ramp or elevator. In 2011, the World Health Organization and the World Bank jointly published a report estimating that about 15% of the world's population lives with some sort of disability. This represents over one billion people on the planet who will potentially become your customer and use your products. And this is only considering permanent disabilities, such as being legally blind or deaf. Disabilities can also be temporary (i.e. cataract), or situational (i.e. being distracted and looking elsewhere). Considering the accessibility of your product is the humane thing to do, and it will offer a better usability for everyone, thus increasing your market share. For example, if you design your product in such a way that it can be used with one hand, it will be accessible to people who have one arm. It will also be accessible to people who temporarily have an arm cast, as well as people currently holding a baby, a drink, or a handrail. The population is also aging, so while you might not have any disability today, maybe you're only a few years away from having rheumatoid arthritis making your fine motor control difficult and painful, or from experiencing a decrease of your vision and hearing (see Don Norman's piece for *Fast Company*, pointing out that the world is designed against the elderly[3]; Norman, 2019). Even before growing old, you might one day experience burnout at your job, making it difficult for you to concentrate on the long blocks of text explaining how to use a new appliance once you're finally home after a strenuous day. If these elements are not enough to convince you or your manager, then maybe consider the rise of accessibility lawsuits. As UX designer Reginé Gilbert points out in her book *Inclusive Design for a Digital World* (2019), there were 2,258 web accessibility lawsuits filed in the United States in 2018, nearly tripling as compared to the year before. Many governments today have legislation requiring that people with disabilities can enjoy equal access to public services, such as the Americans with Disabilities Act (ADA), or the European Accessibility Act. Furthermore, making a product accessible won't necessarily increase your production time as long as you plan for it in advance. There are a lot of resources online that can guide you, such as usability.gov, webaccessibility.com, or the *Dos and don'ts on designing for accessibility*[4] (Pun, 2016).

Think about disability not as a person's impairment, but as the way society is organized and products are built that create unnecessary barriers to use and enjoyment. Gilbert calls this the "social model of disability." Our human-built environment often discriminates against people with disabilities because of bad or careless design. Similarly, design can discriminate against underrepresented minorities or women. For example, if you're designing a technology tool that unnecessarily requires constant Internet connection, it will discriminate against people living in remote areas with bad Internet coverage, or people who cannot afford an Internet subscription. This is what we call *systemic* discrimination: systems built by some humans end up not being inclusive to all. Most of the time, it's not intentional. We all have our "unawareness" spots. As we saw earlier, perception is subjective. Depending on your gender, the color of your skin, the neighborhood you grew up in, if you're able-bodied or disabled, you will experience the world differently. When we forget that our perspective on the environment or a product is not universal, we fall for the "egocentric bias," which is very common. Let's say that you're designing a soap dispenser that automatically releases some soap when it detects a hand placed underneath it. You have tight deadlines and thus neglect to UX test the product and only test it internally. It seems to work well when tested by the different people on your team, everyone is satisfied, and you release the product. Except that, because

---

[3] https://www.fastcompany.com/90338379/i-wrote-the-book-on-user-friendly-design-what-i-see-today-horrifies-me.
[4] https://accessibility.blog.gov.uk/2016/09/02/dos-and-donts-on-designing-for-accessibility/.

your team is exclusively composed of white people, it didn't occur to you to test it with different skin tones and it turns out that the soap dispenser doesn't detect darker skins. Which you only discover because a Black person posts a video on social media showing that your soap dispenser doesn't detect their hand while it works with a white napkin (this is a real story, at least the social media part of it). Because you hurried up to meet your deadline and maybe save some money during production now your product is not usable by the majority of the people in the world and it's almost guaranteed that you will have a justified public relation (PR) backlash to clean up.

The same type of stories goes for life-saving health devices, access to housing, or education. In her thoroughly researched book *Invisible Women* (2019), Caroline Criado Perez dissects how women are often discriminated against by systems mostly created by men. Take the example of car design: did you know that it wasn't until 2011 that the United States started to use female crash-test dummies? Until then, the most commonly used dummy was the "average male:" 1.77 m tall and weighing 76 kg (i.e. 5.8 feet tall and about 167 pounds). Which means that most women and anyone diverging significantly from the "average male" were at higher risk of injury in the case of collision.

We're only humans. A few people on a team, especially a homogeneous team, simply won't be able to account for the experience of every type of user. Having a UX mindset also means accounting for our own biases and designing with inclusion in mind, which in turn entails striving to build diverse and inclusive teams. Among the guiding principles for inclusive design that she provides, Gilbert (2019) encourages readers to balance their biases, to ask themselves what their lenses are.

> Your lenses are always there, and they influence how you see the world. These could be inherited (e.g. race, gender, nationality), developed (political views or religious perspectives), or behavioral (How do you approach problems? Whom do you get advice from? Where do you find news?). (p. 102)

It's absolutely normal to have these lenses and to be biased. Everyone has, and everyone is. But in our global market today, it *really* is not good enough to be sorry after the fact and say as an excuse that we didn't know. Realizing that we don't know should now be common knowledge. Learn to identify your biases and lenses, put together an inclusive team, hire accessibility and inclusion specialists, and invite a diverse pool of participants to your UX tests. Building for diversity, equity, and inclusion is not necessarily easy, but it's certainly not impossible. It's just another design challenge, and one that should be core to what UX experts and advocates do.

I would also argue that inclusion is warranted within the UX community itself. While UX professionals are often advocating for inclusion, the voices of marginalized UX professionals are ironically not heard as much as other voices. As UX designer and founder of Humanity Centered (hmntycntrd.com), Vivianne Castillo rightfully points out, it's easier to "like the idea of caring about people" than "actually care about people" (Castillo, 2017). Designing for equity and being inclusive require conscious effort, including from UX experts.

One more thing: do not believe that artificial intelligence (AI) can succeed in making the world more inclusive where humans have failed (or haven't tried hard enough). It's not because AI is not human that it's not biased. AI uses big data to make its predictions. The problem with the data is that it's completely skewed by human biases. As Cathy O'Neil says in her book *Weapons of Math Destruction* (2016), a model has "blind" spots (i.e. unawareness spots) reflecting the biases and lenses of its creators. Take the example of the AI tool for recruitment that Amazon built in the mid-2010s to supposedly preselect the best resumes for a position without being biased like humans would when we make such decisions. Turns out, it actually discriminated against women because it made its selection based on past resumes and hires, which, as you might have guessed, were predominantly male. Thus, the AI concluded that being male was probably a good predictive criterion for hire. As AI experts commonly say: "garbage in, garbage out." The problem is that it's extremely difficult to anticipate how your data can be biased in the first place. AI is thus biased in a very opaque way. This is how discrimination can be perpetuated and aggravated with AI in ways we might not realize (or want to realize) until after the harm is done. As O'Neil brilliantly points out: "Big Data processes codify the past. They do not invent the future. Doing that requires moral imagination, and that's something only humans can provide" (p. 204).

The barriers of access in our society are not natural; they are human-made. Discrimination is often systemic. If we care about equity and justice, we must identify those systemic barriers. UX experts must strive to design for inclusion.

5.6 The Ethics of UX

As we saw in this chapter, design can exclude or take advantage of people. Having a UX mindset implies placing users' best interests in the forefront. It means caring about accessibility, inclusion, and overall respect for the people using the products we make, as well as their privacy in the age of data collection. It can of course be a win-win balance between users and the business, but it should never be profits over humans. To make our care for humans clear, I would argue that UX professionals should formally pledge to follow a code of ethics when they graduate or accept a UX job, along the lines of the Association for Computing Machinery (ACM) Code of Ethics and Professional Conduct,[5] or the Code of Professional Conduct of the User Experience Professionals Association (UXPA).[6] That being said, it wouldn't be fair to place all the ethical responsibilities on UX practitioners. After all, in most cases, they don't have a lot of weight in the decision making when the UX maturity of the company they work for is not very advanced (which is the case for the large majority of companies). It's sadly commonplace for UX professionals to identify a dark pattern or gray area practice, point it out to their managers, only to hear back from leadership that they don't give a sh*t. "Our competitors are doing it and it seems to work well for them, so why shouldn't we?" In the absence of regulations (which can be very tricky for lawmakers to navigate in the case of shady practices) or public pressure, our capitalistic economy is not particularly rewarding ethical practices. At least not in the short term. In the long term, it makes a strong business case to be respectful of customers and nurture a long-lasting trust relationship. So what should UX professionals do when they are asked to implement a dark or gray pattern, or dismissed when they ask for accessibility features to be implemented? Technically, if they pledged to follow a code of ethics, should they just refuse to do the job? Should they resign in protest? It's not realistic nor would it be fair to expect these professionals, who have an average salary and aren't decision makers in an organization for the most part, to carry all the ethical responsibilities. They should be the ones raising red and orange flags, but the ethical responsibility has to be shared across the whole company, and increases at higher hierarchy levels.

Advocating for a genuine UX mindset can help advancing ethics in design and society for everyone. Make no mistake: you are likely forgotten in some designs, or even discriminated against by some systems. And even if you're among the very happy few who aren't disfavored by design today, you will very likely be as you grow older. We all gain from pushing for UX values as long as they can be understood and recognized.

---

[5] https://www.acm.org/code-of-ethics.
[6] https://uxpa.org/uxpa-code-of-professional-conduct/.

Conclusion

We are nearing the end of our journey together, and I would like to warmly thank you for reading this book all the way until here. My goal was to humbly contribute in promoting the real values of UX, and why we can ultimately all benefit from them. As I hope I made clear, UX is not just about knowledge, expertise, tools, or processes; UX is a philosophy above all else. It entails caring about how all users will experience a product, instead of caring about design for itself, or prioritizing business goals. It's about shifting from our egocentric vision of product development to factor in and prioritize the humans whom we are designing for.

In a nutshell, the four most important UX mindset pillars to remember are:

- **UX implies placing users at the center of what we do**: We do not create and refine a product in a silo; we primarily care about solving users' problems and thus need listening skills, compassion, and respect for the people who will use our products.
- **UX is grounded in science**: In order to design for humans, we need to understand humans and how their mind—where an experience happens—works. We use knowledge from cognitive and social sciences, and we regularly test our product using a scientific approach to avoid biasing our conclusions.
- **UX is a team-based process**: In a team effort, we start by empathizing with users and understanding their problems, then we ideate, prototype, test, implement, retest, and keep refining the product with users.
- **UX is about caring for users' best interests and ethics**: Having a UX mindset is incompatible with the use of dark and shady patterns. It also implies a care for inclusive design that will be safe for all.

There are many paths to UX. If you're interested in becoming a UX professional, you can come from academia, or come from practice. You might have more of an industrial design lens, or more of an interaction design lens, or more of a usability and research lens. Everyone is invited, as long as UX values are respected and defended. However, it does take time and effort to become a UX expert as understanding how humans behave and think in order to offer them the best experience possible is not an easy task. It takes years of practice, study, and/or research to start having a better sense of what UX implies. We owe our users this effort but I guarantee you that it's worth it. It's not only satisfying to offer a great experience to people and improve their lives, it's also good business and it will foster a long-lasting trust relationship with your customers.

You won't become the next successful entrepreneur by merely copying what was done in the past. The world constantly changes, people's needs and desires evolve, and challenges are never the same. But you will make a difference by having a human-centered experience mindset. Unlike technology, human brain capabilities, performance, and limitations do not constantly change. Having a good understanding of human factors psychology and UX methodologies will never get old, and it will also be your best ally. And as consumers ourselves, we expect the technology we use to make our lives easier, not more frustrating, which is why we should demand companies and public services to strive for better UX, including ethics and equity.

There is no one recipe for great and successful products, but there are ingredients and a process that can foster innovation and long-lasting commercial success. Care for the humans and their environment. Offer solutions to *their* problems. Find how you will enrich people's lives for the best, and more importantly, *why* it matters to them.

The future is humanistic; it's for us to design it.

Acknowledgments

This book was surprisingly very hard to write, especially during a pandemic. Without the support of my friends, family, and mentors, I would still be stressfully staring at a blank page. More specifically, I would like to warmly thank Laura Taylor for her incredibly detailed and insightful feedback and for her great illustrations, María Capel for her indefectible support, the well-needed hikes, and her wonderful "UX mindset pillars" illustration (and thanks Rubén for the bread!). I wish to thank Katherine Isbister, Anne McLaughlin, Anouk Ben-Tchavtachvadze, Fran Blumberg, Scott Jenson, Fred Markus, Mary Bihr, and Darren Sugg for their precious feedback. I would also like to thank Alan Cooper and Jonathan Korman for their feedback and the insightful and passionate discussions, and Sue Cooper for her help. Lastly I'd like to thank my editor Sean Connelly for his patience. Thank you for reading these lines!

Glossary

Accessibility: it's about making a product accessible to people with disabilities. A disability can be permanent (e.g. being legally blind), temporary (e.g. cataract), or situational (e.g. being distracted).

Affordance: there's an affordance when the characteristics of an object facilitate our interaction with it (such as a handle helping us pull a door open). Cognitive affordances (i.e. signifiers) are the shapes, labels, or metaphors that convey the functionality of an element, and how to use it.

Cognitive science: the scientific study of mental processes such as attention, memory, and reasoning allowing us to acquire knowledge, maintain and manipulate it, and overall make sense of the world. It's the backbone of the human factors field and UX, since an experience is what happens in people's minds as they interact with a product. Our mental processes have great limitations, which we are mostly unaware of: perception is subjective, memory is fallible, and attentional resources are scarce.

Dark pattern: term coined by Harry Brignull. It's a deceptive design that was created intentionally with the purpose of favoring business profits at the expense of users.

Design thinking: creative process focusing on innovation that heavily relies on human-centered design.

Emotional design: According to Donald Norman, any design has three levels of processing: visceral, behavioral, and reflective, which interlace emotion and cognition.

Engage-ability: the ability of a product or system to be engaging (mostly, the motivation and emotions elicited by the product, especially entertainment systems like video games).

Ethics: in UX, it's about considering the impact of a design on a user, a specific group or community, and on society at large. Accounting for inclusion and accessibility, and avoiding dark patterns and shady practices are part of the UX mindset.

Experience: refers to what happens when the user interacts with a product, a system, or a service, broadly speaking. An experience happens in people's minds as they interact with a product. Thus, we cannot design an experience; we design *for* an experience.

Field study: research conducted outside of a UX lab to empathize with users and understand their goals by making direct observations as they go about their job or other daily occupations, interviewing them, and spending time with them.

Fitts's law: it's a HCI model that predicts the time it will take a human to point at an element (such as using a mouse to point at an icon on a graphical user interface, or reaching a button with a finger).

Flowchart (or flow diagram): it's a diagram clearly mapping out how a user gets to different parts of the product, and where from, thus defining the route and the means by which users can take that route.

Focus group: it's an exploratory tool in UX research that consists of inviting potential users to discuss how they feel about a competitive product, or what they would expect from a new product in development. The idea is to uncover their problems, their needs, their desires, and their expectations.

Gamification: it's a way of approaching the design of a system or service to be playful. However, the gamification approach often too narrowly focuses on extrinsic rewards that games provide (e.g. point scoring, badges, or competition) instead of embracing the full engage-ability potential of video games, such as intrinsic motivation (see Hodent, 2020).

Gestalt principles of perception: general laws predicting how simple patterns will be perceived by humans (e.g. law of similarity stating that objects with similar attributes such as shape, pitch, or brightness are grouped together; law of proximity stating that objects that are close to one another in space or time are grouped together).

Heuristic evaluation: it's usually conducted by a usability expert (or, preferentially, several) to evaluate the usability of a prototype or an early version of a product using a set of usability heuristics (i.e. rules of thumb, guidelines).

Hick-Hyman law (also called Hick's law): HCI model for choice reaction time. It posits that the time it takes for a user to make a decision will logarithmically increase with the number of options displayed.

Human-centered design (HCD): iterative methodology used by UX designers. It entails understanding who the targeted users and their goals are first, and then developing prototypes that are tested with users before iterating further and implementing designs. The main goal of HCD is to solve problems that users have. HCD can be used as a synonym for UX design or interaction design.

Human-computer interaction (HCI): branch of human factors field that studies how humans interact with digital environments more specifically. Its main purpose is to improve people's lives with technology.

Human factors field: aims at increasing the ease of use, comfort, security, and even pleasure when humans interact with objects or systems. It applies cognitive science knowledge. Human factors guidelines and principles account for human capabilities, performance, and limitations.

Implicit biases: biases that impact our perception, thoughts, and decision making without our awareness (e.g. hindsight bias, confirmation bias, curse of knowledge, egocentric bias, overconfidence bias, loss aversion, status quo bias).

Inclusion: Inclusion is about making sure that no one is excluded from a product, service, or system. It entails first identify our own biases (i.e. the lenses by which with subjectively see the world), identify the systemic discriminations of a system creating barriers of access or opportunity (i.e. the populations who aren't accounted for in the design of a system or product), and breaking down those barriers.

Industrial design: the practice of designing physical objects manufactured by mass production.

Information architecture: it's about organizing the content and features of a product to help users understand the product and accomplish their goals.

Innovation: it's an invention that meets a market and people's goals. There are three overlapping criteria for innovation, according to industrial designer and IDEO chair Tim Brown (2019): feasibility (what's functionally possible within the material and time constraints), viability (sustainable business model), and desirability (what makes sense to people and for people).

Interaction design: broadly speaking, it's about determining how users will interact with a product. Interaction design also designates the practice of designing interactive digital products (abbreviated as "IxD"). It can be used as a synonym for human-centered design or UX design for interactive products.

Lean UX: Lean UX is about fostering a UX mindset within a Lean approach to product development management. The Lean approach favors fast iteration and customer insights. The idea is typically to first build a MVP as fast as possible, get it out of the door, and see how people use it, so that the product can be refined with actual user feedback.

Mental model: it's the conceptual model (or mental representation) that we have about how a system works depending on our prior knowledge and understanding of the system. Users' mental model of a product can differ from the mental model of the creators of the product, which often leads to users not understanding how it works and being frustrated, and creators not understanding why this is happening.

Motivation: motivation is what makes humans (and other animals) accomplish actions. There is currently no one theory of motivation that can account for all human behaviors. The main types of motivation useful in UX design is extrinsic motivation (what we do in order to gain a reward external to the activity) and intrinsic motivation (activities that we do for the pleasure of doing them). The most reliable theory for intrinsic motivation is the self-determination theory (SDT), which posits that we are more intrinsically motivated when accomplishing activities satisfying our needs for competence (i.e. control and progression), autonomy (self-expression and meaningful choices), and relatedness (e.g. cooperating with others). Other types of motivations that can influence our behavior are implicit motivation (i.e. impulses) and individual needs (i.e. personality).

MVP: minimum viable product, the smallest version of a functional product that takes the least amount of effort to put together, yet can yield very insightful feedback from actual users.

OCEAN personality test (also called Big Five): is the most reliable personality test currently available (unlike the Briggs-Myers test that is not validated scientifically and is thus useless). It measures five personality traits: Openness to experience, Conscientiousness, Extraversion, Agreeableness, and Neuroticism.

Pareto principle: also known as the "80/20 rule," it posits that 20% of the variables in a system are responsible for 80% of the results. For example, 80% of your users' interaction with your system will concern only 20% of the system features.

Persona: it's a method about distilling all of the insights gathered from real people during field studies into a profile with specific goals, desires, expectations, routines, and even a specific name and photo, so that it can be used to support the design thinking process.

Product: refers to anything users interact with to attain goals, or to be entertained. It can be a physical object, a digital object, a system, or a service.

Prototype: mocked-up version of an idea for flows and layouts that are created to try them out before building the real thing. It enables nontechnical people to quickly create "real" looking interfaces without requiring implementation from an engineer. They are intended to be a high-level representation of the intended design focused on functionality and interaction, without getting caught up in the details of its "look and feel."

Scientific method: a standardized and rigorous way of acquiring knowledge. The scientific method is a way to acquire knowledge using careful methodologies to account for human biases and errors. UX research uses the scientific method.

Shady practice: it's a design intentionally created with the purpose of exploiting human flaws and biases to increase business profits, while the benefits for users aren't clear (or aren't the main focus). Contrary to a dark pattern, a shady practice is not technically deceiving users.

UI: user interface, the part of a product or system that users perceive and interact with.

Usability: quality attribute assessing the ease of use of a product or system; its *ability* to be *used*. Usability is what we aim for in HCI: making a product easy to use (i.e. effective), efficient, and satisfying for all users as they interact with it in various situations.

Users: the humans interacting with a product, who may or may not also be customers.

User journey: it's a method about defining what users want to do (i.e. problem to solve) and their expectations, how they would go about accomplishing their goal, and what they will do, think, and feel along the way. It's the big picture of what users will experience with a product ecosystem.

UX: User experience is a term coined by Donald Norman and is best seen as a mindset. It implies caring about the *experience* that *users* have or will have with a product and its ecosystem (i.e. the whole user journey with a product, brand, and company). It's about shifting from the subjective and necessarily biased point of view of the small number of people working on a product, to adopt the point of view of all potential users (the "target audience") with the intention of solving their problems and offering them the best experience possible while having their best interests in mind. The UX mindset is about four main pillars: being human-centered, being grounded in science, having a team-based process, and being benevolent.

UX designers: experts in designing *for* an experience having users' goals in mind, using human factors psychology and human-computer interaction principles, and having an iterative process called human-centered design. UX design designates a generalist role encompassing all the following tasks: understanding users and their needs, generating ideas to solve users' problems (ideation phase), prototyping, testing with actual users, iterating, and refining the design until it's ready for implementation. UX design focuses on *why* users should care about the product and *how* it should work.

UX maturity: it's the level of UX understanding and UX expertise and practices in place at a company. At the lowest level of maturity, UX is rejected and misunderstood. At the highest level, UX is a culture across the company.

UX researchers: experts in conducting studies or analyses using the scientific method to understand users and evaluate their experience with a product objectively. UX researchers are specifically trained in determining the adequate research methodology, designing rigorous experimental protocols, preparing and running the study, collecting data, and analyzing results without introducing any biases, or at least by controlling for them.

UX strategists: UX experts who have evolved to a managing role. They typically advocate for UX, manage other UX experts, establish a UX strategy, and advance UX maturity in a company.

UX test: generic term for user evaluative research methodologies. A UX test generally aims at evaluating if the product in development is usable and solve users' problems. The main test used is the "usability test," which typically consists of observing users as they accomplish their goals with a product to identify and understand all the pain points that users encounter.

Von Restorff effect: predicts that the more an element stands out from its surroundings, the better we remember it.

Wireframe: it's the high level visualization of the skeleton of a website or an application. Like a schematic or blueprint, it communicates the envisioned page layout, information hierarchy, user flow, and interactions.

Some Recommended Readings

- *The Design of Everyday Things*, by Don Norman
- *Don't Make Me Think*, by Steve Krug
- *Designing with the Mind in Mind*, by Jeff Johnson
- *A Life in Error*, by James Reason
- *Introduction to Human Factors*, by Nancy Stone, Alex Chaparro, Joseph Keebler, Barbara Chaparro, and Daniel McConnell
- *The UX Book*, by Rex Harston and Pardha Pyla
- *Inclusive Design for a Digital World*, by Reginé Gilbert
- *Invisible Women*, by Caroline Criado Perez
- *Calling Bullshit*, by Carl Bergstrom and Jevin West
- *Thinking, Fast and Slow*, by Daniel Kahneman

Some Recommended Websites

- IXDA.org
- Interaction-Design.org
- NNgroup.com
- HFES.org
- ACM.org
- DarkPatterns.org
- EthicalGames.org
- DesignThatMatters.org

References

Abraham, A. (2018). *The Neuroscience of Creativity*. Cambridge: Cambridge University Press.

Allerton, M., & Blake, W. (2008). The "Party Drug" Crystal Methamphetamine: Risk Factor for the Acquisition of HIV. *The Permanente Journal, 12*, 56–58.

Ariely, D. (2008). *Predictably Irrational: The Hidden Forces That Shape Our Decisions*. New York: Harper Collins.

Atkinson, R. C., & Shiffrin, R. M. (1968). Human memory: A proposed system and its control processes. In Spence, K. W., & Spence, J. T. (Eds.), *The Psychology of Learning and Motivation* (Volume 2). New York: Academic Press, 89–195.

Bergstrom, C.T., & West, J.D (2020). *Calling Bullshit: The Art of Skepticism in a Data-Driven World*. New York: Random House.

Brown, T. (2019). *Change by Design: How Design Thinking Transforms Organizations and Inspires Innovation, Revised and Updated*. Chicago, IL: Harper Business.

Castillo, V. (2017). *Part III: Greed Over Humanity*. Retrieved from https://uxdesign.cc/part-iii-why-most-conversations-in-tech-about-diversity-are-bullshit-and-what-to-do-about-it-b1db8900fce7 (Accessed October 13th, 2021).

Cooper, A. (2004). *The Inmates Are Running the Asylum: Why High Tech Products Drive Us Crazy and How to Restore the Sanity*. Indianapolis, IN: Sams Publishing.

Criado Perez, C. (2019). *Invisible Women: Data Bias in a World Designed for Men*. New York: Abrams Press.

Dickerson, J. (2013). Attention to Detail, a Focus on Immersion, and the Desire Constantly Improve His Products Made Walt Disney One of the Earliest Designers of User Experience. *UX Matters*. Retrieved from https://uxmag.com/articles/walt-disney-the-worlds-first-ux-designer (Accessed June 11, 2021).

Dreyfuss, H. (2003). *Designing for People* (originally published in 1955). New York: Allworth Press.

Fitts, P.M., & Jones, R.E. (1947). *Analysis of Factors Contributing to 460 "Pilot Error" Experiences in Operating Aircraft Controls (Report No. TSEAA-694-12)*. Dayton, OH: Aero Medical Laboratory, Air Materiel Command, U.S. Air Force.

Foddy, B. (2016) "The pleasures and perils of operant behavior", In Heather, N. and Segal, G. (Eds), *Addiction and Choice: Rethinking the Relationship*. Oxford, UK: Oxofrd University Press, pp. 49-65.

Garrett, J.J. (2011). *The Elements of User Experience: User-Centered Design for the Web and Beyond*, 2nd Edition. New York: Pearson Education.

Garrett, J.J. (2021). I Helped Pioneer UX Design. What I See Today Disturbs Me. *Fast Company*. Retrieved from https://www.fastcompany.com/90642462/i-helped-pioneer-ux-design-what-i-see-today-horrifies-me (Accessed June 3, 2021).

Gibbons, S. (2016). *Design Thinking 101*. NN group. Retrieved from https://www.nngroup.com/articles/design-thinking/ (Accessed June 11, 2021).

Gilbert, R.M. (2019). *Inclusive Design for a Digital World: Designing with Accessibility in Mind*. New York: Springer.

Goodwin, K. (2009). *Designing for the Digital Age: How to Create Human-Centered Products and Services*. Indianapolis, IN: Wiley.

Hartson, R. (2003). Cognitive, Physical, Sensory, and Functional Affordances in Interaction Design. *Interaction Design*, *22*, 315–338.

Hartson, R. & Pyla, P. (2012). *The UX Book: Process and Guidelines for Ensuring a Quality User Experience*. Waltham, MA: Morgan Kaufmann/Elsevier.

Hodent, C. (2017). *The Gamer's Brain: How Neuroscience and UX Can Impact Video Game Design*. Boca Raton, FL: CRC Press.

Hodent, C. (2019). *Ethics in the Videogame Industry: A Mythbusting and Scientific Approach*. Retrieved from https://celiahodent.com/ethics-in-the-videogame-industry/ (Accessed June 11, 2021).

Hodent, C. (2020). *The Psychology of Video Games*. Abingdon: Routledge.

Jenson, S. (2020). *Assertive Instincts*. Retrieved from https://jenson.org/instincts/. (Accessed September 1st, 2021).

Johnson, J. (2010). *Designing with the Mind in Mind: Simple Guide to Understanding User Interface Design Guidelines*. Burlington: Elsevier.

Kahneman, D. (2011). *Thinking, Fast and Slow*. New York: Farrar, Straus and Giroux.

Kelley, T. & Kelley, D. (2013). *Creative Confidence: Unleashing the Creative Potential Within Us All*. New York: Crown Business.

Kelley, T. & Littman, J. (2001). *The Art of Innovation: Lessons in Creativity from IDEO, America's Leading Design Firm*. New York: Doubleday.

Kjaer, T.W, Bertelsen, C., Piccini, P., Brooks, D., Alving, J., & Lou, H.C. (2002). Increased Dopamine Tone During Meditation-Induced Change of Consciousness. *Cognitive Brain Research*, *13*, 255–259.

Klein, L. (2018). *UX for Lean Startups: Faster, Smarter User Experience Research and Design*. Sebastopol, CA: O'Reilly.

Koepp, M.J., Gunn, R.N., Lawrence, A.D., Cunningham, V.J., Dagher, A., Jones, T., Brooks, D.J., Bench, C.J., & Grasby, P.M. (1998). Evidence for Striatal Dopaminerelease During a Video Game. *Nature*, *393*, 266–268.

Korman, J. (2012). *Whither "User Experience Design"?* Retrieved from https://boxesandarrows.com/this-thing-that-we-do/ (Accessed July 3rd 2021).

Krug, S. (2014). *Don't Make Me Think, Revisited: A Common Sense Approach to Web Usability*. Third edition. San Francisco, CA: New Riders, Peachpit, Pearson Education.

Laurel, B. (2013). *Computers as Theatre*, 2nd edition. New York: Pearson Education.

Marmaras, N., Poulakakis, G., & Papakostopoulos, V. (1999). Ergonomic Design in Ancient Greece. *Applied Ergonomics, 30,* 361–368.

Medlock, M.C., Wixon, D., Terrano, M., Romero, R., & Fulton, B. (2002). Using the RITE method to improve products: A definition and a case study. *Presented at the Usability Professionals Association 2002,* Orlando, FL.

Merholz, P., Wilkens, T., Schauer, B, & Verba, D. (2008). *Subject to Change: Creating Great Products & Services for an Uncertain World.* Sebastopol, CA: O'Reilly.

Nielsen, J. (1994). Enhancing the explanatory power of usability heuristics. *Proceeding of ACM CHI'94 Conf*erence, Boston, MA, April 24–28, 152–158.

Nielsen, J. (2000). *Why You Only Need to Test with 5 Users.* NN Group. Retrieved from https://www.nngroup.com/articles/why-you-only-need-to-test-with-5-users/ (Accessed June 11, 2021).

Nielsen, J. (2006a). *Corporate UX Maturity: Stages 1–4.* NN Group. Retrieved from https://www.nngroup.com/articles/ux-maturity-stages-1-4/ (Accessed May 8, 2021).

Nielsen, J. (2006b). *Corporate UX Maturity: Stages 5–8.* NN Group. Retrieved from https://www.nngroup.com/articles/ux-maturity-stages-5-8/ (Accessed May 8, 2021).

Nielsen, J. (2012). *Usability 101: Introduction to Usability.* NN Group. Retrieved from https://www.nngroup.com/articles/usability-101-introduction-to-usability/ (Accessed May 8, 2021).

Norman, D.A. (2005). *Emotional Design: Why We Love (or Hate) Everyday Things.* New York: Basic Books.

Norman, D.A. (2013). *The Design of Everyday Things, Revised and Expanded Edition.* New York: Basic Books.

Norman, D. (2019). *I Wrote the Book on User-Friendly Design. What I See Today Horrifies Me.* Fast Company. Retrieved from https://www.fastcompany.com/90338379/i-wrote-the-book-on-user-friendly-design-what-i-see-today-horrifies-me (Accessed May 8, 2021).

O'Neil, C. (2016). *Weapons of Math Destruction: How Big Data Increases Inequality and Threatens Democracy.* New York: Crown Books.

Pernice, K., Gibbons, S., Moran, K., & Whitenton, K. *The 6 Levels of UX Maturity.* NN Group. Retrieved from https://www.nngroup.com/articles/ux-maturity-model/ (Accessed June 14, 2021).

Pittenger, D.J. (1993). The Utility of the Myers-Briggs Type Indicator. *Review of Educational Research, 63,* 467–488. https://journals.sagepub.com/doi/abs/10.3102/00346543063004467.

Pun, K. (2016). *Dos and Don'ts on Designing for Accessibility,* UK.Gov. Retrieved from https://accessibility.blog.gov.uk/2016/09/02/dos-and-donts-on-designing-for-accessibility/ (Accessed June 14, 2021).

Reason, J. (2013). *A Life in Error: From Little Slips to Big Disasters.* Farnham: Ashgate.

Ries, E. (2011). *The Lean Startup: How Today's Entrepreneurs Use Continuous Innovation to Create Radically Successful Businesses.* New York: Crown Business.

Ryan, R. M., & Deci, E. L. (2000). Self-determination theory and the facilitation of intrinsic motivation, social development, and well-being. *American Psychologist, 55,* 68–78.

Stone, N.J., Chaparro, A., Keebler, J.R., Chaparro, B.S., & McConnell, D.S. (2018). *Introduction to Human Factors: Applying Psychology to Design.* Boca Raton, FL: CRC Press.

Thaler, R.H., & Sunstein, C.S. (2008). *Nudge: Improving Decisions about Health, Wealth, and Happiness.* New Haven & London: Yale University Press.

Wertheimer, M. (1923). Untersuchungen zur Lehre der Gestalt II. *Psychol Forsch, 4,* 301–350. Translation published as Laws of Organization in Perceptual Forms, In Ellis, W. A. (1938). *Source Book of Gestalt Psychology.* London: Routledge and Kegan Paul, 71–88.

Index